THE NARROW BRIDGE

THE NARROW BRIDGE

Beyond the Holocaust

Isaac Neuman

with Michael Palencia-Roth

UNIVERSITY OF ILLINOIS PRESS

URBANA AND CHICAGO

Library of Congress Cataloging-in-Publication Data
Neuman, Isaac, 1922–
The narrow bridge: beyond the Holocaust / Isaac Neuman;
with Michael Palencia-Roth.
p.   cm.
1. Neuman, Isaac, 1922–
2. Jews—Poland—Zdunska Wola—Biography.
3. Holocaust, Jewish (1939–1945)—Poland—Zdunska Wola—
Personal narratives.
4. Zdunska Wola (Poland)—Biography.
I. Palencia-Roth, Michael.
II. Title.
DS135.P63N485   2000
940.53'18092—dc21   99-006847
C 5 4 3 2 1

To the memory of my father and mother,
my sisters and my brother,
and my teacher, Reb Mendel—
all of whom died in the Holocaust.
   —I.N.

In memory of my mother,
Shirley Roth de Palencia (December 3, 1910–December 18, 1991).
   —M.P-R.

Contents

PREFACE   ix

Part 1: Before the Ghetto
  1. Cheder Years   3
  2. Reb Mendel   19
  3. The Gate of Tears   39

Part 2: In the Ghetto
  4. Hanukkah in a Monastery   55
  5. The Pact   65
  6. Purim Revenge   72
  7. Shlomo's Last Prayer   83
  8. The Judenälteste of Zdunska Wola   95

Part 3: In the Camps
  9. My Brother's Keeper, Part 1   109
  10. Unleavened Bread   123
  11. My Brother's Keeper, Part 2   137

Part 4: Legacies
  12. Mottl's Torah   155
  13. Rachel   162
  14. Yom Hashoah   173

Afterword   187

GLOSSARY   191
INDEX   197

Illustrations follow page 122

Preface

In April 1995 I underwent my second coronary bypass operation. For the first seventy-two hours afterward, no one really knew whether or not I would survive. As I lay in the Cleveland Clinic, waiting to see which path my body would follow, I became angry and depressed. This, I knew, was a normal reaction, but somehow that knowledge was of little comfort. The hospital chaplain came to see me each day. On the third day, knowing that I was a rabbi, he offered to get me some Jewish music from the hospital music library.

"Would you have a mystical song called 'Tanya'?" I asked. "Or a modern rendition of it? It is used for the liturgical portion of the Yom Kippur afternoon service."

"We have a selection of High Holiday music as well as Hasidic music," he answered. "If we have it, I will send it up to you."

Later that day, the tape he had selected arrived at my room. When I saw it, I almost sent it back, for I thought that he had made a mistake. The cassette was of songs by a contemporary Israeli singer and had nothing to do with the High Holy Days. But my wife Eva said, "Let's listen to it anyway. It can't hurt."

On hearing the first song, my anger and depression broke, scattered by the melody as a cloud is scattered by wind. I began to cry and then to sing the melody along with the singer. I needed that song and only that song, although it was not what I had requested.

Unwittingly, the chaplain had sent me a song of the traditional morning prayer that every Jew should recite upon arising. It was with this melody that my grandmother used to wake me whenever I stayed overnight in her apartment in our hometown of Zdunska Wola, Poland. Coming into my room, she would sing the song until I fully awakened. Then she would have me wash my hands. And then, together, holding hands and clapping at the appropriate places, we would sing the song again. This simple melody, called "Modeh-ani," has stayed with me for all of my life:

> Modeh-ani, lefanechu
> Melech chai vekayam
> Schechezarto bee nishmosi,
> Bechemlo,
> Rabbo emunasachu.
>
> [I give thanks to you, everlasting king,
> That you have returned to me my soul,
> With compassion.
> Great is your faithfulness.]

I have often thought that many of the songs to which Jewish children have sung and danced over the ages have been interrupted and silenced and now float around the universe, waiting for new singers. The Hasidic masters say that whenever a silenced song is sung again, it is restored to its proper place in the universe. And the soul of the singer is lifted up as well.

As I listened to that old, remembered melody being now interpreted by a contemporary Israeli singer, the world of my grandmother flooded back into my consciousness, the world of Zdunska Wola into which I was born in 1922 and which by 1945 had been shattered forever. I witnessed its oblivion—by decrees, by bombs, by occupation, by deportations, by holocaust, by death, by loss of memory. On that April morning in 1995, through the lilting melody of "Modeh-ani," I felt that I was waking up in Zdunska Wola, anticipating the aromas of the Sabbath, feeling the plush bedspread under my fingertips, and yielding to the callused firmness of my grandmother's hands as they held mine during the morning prayer song. From other apartments I could hear the sounds of the tenants preparing for the day. I was seven years old again.

The book that follows is an attempt to restore the silenced song of my vanished world and to tell—through the stories of its people—what it was like to live in Zdunska Wola and to live through its destruction. Fragments of many of these stories I have told during my years as a rabbi in Panama and in Alabama, Iowa, Illinois, and East Germany. The stories as a whole I am telling here for the first time, reviving memories too painful to relate for many, many years. But I feel now a special urgency, an obligation not to squander the gift of life after April 1995, a gift made possible by my two sons, David and Ari Mark, who arranged for my operation, and enhanced by Eva and my closest friends.

—ISAAC NEUMAN

PART ONE

BEFORE THE GHETTO

Baltic Sea

o Chojnice

POLAND   BELARUS

Furstenfelde ▪
St. Martin's Cemetery   Kolo   Strykow   ▪ Kartus–Bereza
Camp (Poznan)   o   ▪   o   Zgierz
                Zbaszyn   Lodz
                        Sieradz oo ─ Pabianice
GERMANY   ▪ Gross Rosen   Zdunska Wola
                Funfteichen ▪

                CZECH   o Krakow   UKRAINE
                REPUBLIC   ▪ Auschwitz/Birkenau

                Linz
                                SLOVAKIA
        Wels ▪ o▪ Mauthausen
            ▪ Ebensee
        Goisern o
        AUSTRIA   HUNGARY

                                ┌─────────────────────┐
                                │ ▪ Concentration Camp │
                                └─────────────────────┘

O N E

Cheder Years

Jews first came to Zdunska Wola in the mid-eighteenth century, and the first weavers came in 1816. My town thus became a manufacturing center, our factories subcontracting for larger ones in the nearby city of Lodz. Zdunska Wola was not one of the fabled cities of Polish Jewry: It was not Lublin or Kracow or Warsaw, or even Lodz. Although it did have a yeshiva, it was not a great talmudic academy. It was not the birthplace of the Ba'al Shem Tov or any other famous Hasidic masters. But, like many shtetls in Poland (shtetl is the Yiddish diminutive identifying "towns," where Jews and non-Jews lived side by side in sometimes uneasy harmony), Zdunska Wola was a spiritual community, both for me and for the ten thousand other Jews who lived there. The remainder of the twenty-eight thousand inhabitants consisted of Poles and ethnic Germans, but ours was the largest group.

In my community, a boy customarily started cheder (his first religious school) at age three. At that age I had a full head of curly black hair, which I loved very much, which other people often complimented, and which had never been cut. In order to be enrolled in cheder, my father told me, I had to allow the barber to cut my hair. When the time came to take me to the barber, I threw a tantrum. I cried that I wouldn't go if the teacher would not accept me with my long hair.

It was a family crisis. My favorite aunt, Mirele, was called. When she came to our apartment, she asked me to go for a walk with her. She gave me a piece of chocolate and took me to Einstadts Park, a favorite place of mine, both then and all during childhood, for it had a creek, ducks, and goats, a riding path for horses, and a huge tree supposed to be more than six hundred years old. Standing on the little bridge over the creek, I could imagine sailing on a wide river. We walked around the park, talking about this and that. On the way back home she asked me when I would be starting cheder.

"Maybe never," was my reply.

"But how could that be?" she countered. "A Jewish boy who doesn't study Torah will grow up to be a nudnik."

I told her that I didn't want to be a nothing but that the price was too steep. She told me that when I had my hair cut I could leave as many curls as I wished, as long as they were on the sides. These were *peyos*. By the time we reached home she had persuaded me to be a good Jewish boy, to allow my hair to be cut, and to go to cheder.

And so, with hair trimmed but side curls intact, I felt very special on the morning of my first day in cheder. My parents dressed me in my finest clothes, a blue sailor's suit with a round white cap. They then wrapped me in my father's tallis, covering me completely with it so that on the way to cheder I should not see, God forbid, a non-kosher animal like a pig or a horse. I was carried into a droshke or carriage all covered up. In a few minutes we arrived at the cheder, and I had not seen anything *treif*.

The cheder was held in a little room with a low ceiling lighted by a brass oil lamp. The teacher, Reb Arele, his wife Mindel, and all the boys welcomed me warmly. As this was a beginner's cheder, the boys were between three and five. It was the first of many religious schools I would attend continuously from that moment until the Germans invaded Poland fourteen years later. I remember looking around the room and at everyone. I remember seeing a small whip, something like a cat-o'-nine-tails, hanging on the wall up near the ceiling. I remember wondering if I would be whipped and if the teacher, Reb Arele, could reach the whip without standing on a stool. I need not have worried. I never felt that whip, nor did I ever see him use it on any boy.

An ancient and venerated tradition in Judaism tries to ensure that a young boy will love learning. On his first formal exposure to Torah and to the Hebrew alphabet, his teacher will sweeten the letters on the alphabet board with honey, then ask him to lick each letter as he learns it so that sweetness and learning will be forever linked. My own initiation into learning was marked by this sort of sweetness. I remember Reb Arele pulling down from a wall an alphabet board with carved Hebrew letters.

"Can you identify any of these letters?" he asked.

I already knew them, so one by one I did, and for every letter that I identified correctly he gave me a piece of candy. When I finished, my hands were full. I began to put the candy in my school bag in order to eat it at home, but Reb Arele stopped me.

"Not so fast. In our cheder, if someone has good fortune he shares it with his friends. That candy is your good fortune today." So we all sat down, all of us, Reb Arele and his wife, my parents and I, and all the boys, and we all ate the candy. I forgot about my stubbornness and about my lost hair.

My father and mother left. I stayed with Reb Arele and his students. At the end of the day we all sang a song called "Oifn Pripechok" [By the Hearth],* which now, as so much else from those years, echoes with foreboding:

---

*My translation.

1. Oyfn pripetshik brent a fayerl,
   Un in shtub iz heys
   Un der rebe lernt kleyne kinderlekh
   Dem alef-beyz.

2. Zet zhe, kinderlekh, gedenkt zhe, tayere,
   Vos ir lernt do
   Zogt zhe nokh a mol un take nokh a mol:
   Komets-alef: o!

3. Lernt, kinder, mit groys kheyshek,
   Azoy zog ikh aykh on,
   Ver s'vet gikher fun aykh kenen ivre
   Der bakumt a fon.

4. Az ir vet, kinder, elter vern,
   Vet ir aleyn farshteyn,
   Vifl in di oysyes lign trern,
   Un vi fil geveyn.

5. Az ir vet, kinder, dem goles shlepn,
   Oysgemutshet zayn,
   Zolt ir fun di oysyes koyekh shepn,
   Kukt in zey arayn.

[1. In the hearth a fire is burning
   and the room is warm,
   The rebbe teaches little children
   the Aleph—Beth.

2. Look children, remember my dear ones,
   what you are learning now,
   Repeat again and again:
   Komets-alef: o!

3. Study, children, and with great desire,
   this is what I am telling you,
   whoever learns the Hebrew fastest
   will receive a little flag.

4. And when you children grow older,
   You will surely understand
   How many tears in these letters lie,
   And how much weeping.
5. And when you children are driven into exile
   and become exhausted,
   you will draw strength
   when you contemplate these letters.]

The sweetness that marked that day marked also the beginning of my love of learning, a love that has never ended and which, although tinged, as the song hints, with sorrow, has also been a source of strength.

A year or so later, another crisis concerning my education erupted in the family. Because I wasn't making suitable progress in cheder, my father feared that I would not be allowed into the *chumash* cheder (intermediate school) to begin the formal study of the Pentateuch. It was decided—because there were of course no experts in remedial reading at the time—to take me to the rebbe for an evaluation. A few weeks before my fifth birthday, Father and I went to see the rebbe. As everyone did before an audience with the rebbe, my father filled out a *kvitl* (petition sheet) that detailed his concerns. He wrote, I was later told, that he was worried for the future of his son, who seemed to be a slow-learner. The rebbe looked at the kvitl and then at both of us. He motioned for my father to leave the room. Father stepped backward and, with his face always toward the rebbe, as was the custom, moved beyond the threshold. Then he watched the rebbe and me.

"Come closer, Itsekel," the rebbe said and motioned with his hand. I approached. He noticed my nervousness. "Why are you fidgeting?" he asked, putting me on his knee. "Would you like to pull my beard?"

That was exactly what I was wanting to do, but I didn't dare.

"Go ahead," he said. "You have my permission, as long as you do it gently."

And so I pulled the rebbe's beard, running my fingers through the wiry reddish hair. He smiled at me. I smiled at him. We began to talk.

After a bit, the rebbe invited Father to sit next to him and said, "Mordecai, you have a fine son. The only problem is that he is bored with the rote learning in cheder. Take him out, put him in chumash cheder, and everything will be all right."

My father did as the rebbe suggested, and soon there were no more problems with my learning. I adjusted quickly to the Pentateuch and was grateful to be no longer reading nonsense syllables and prayers by rote that I could not understand.

After my fifth birthday my family gave me a chumash *seuda* (party). My relatives and friends came. I was placed on top of a table and asked to answer some questions and give a speech. Although I don't remember what I said, the conversation was supposed to have gone like this:

"Young one, what are you studying?"

"Chumash."

"And what part of chumash?"

"Leviticus."

"And why are you studying Leviticus?"

"Because it begins with a small aleph, and I am a small boy. It is my size."

"And what is Leviticus about?"

"It is about the laws of cleanliness. I like it because I am a clean boy and want to learn more about keeping my mind and body clean."

I don't know now if I actually said all that, but my mother and father always maintained that I did. For them it was a sign that I was destined to study Torah. What I really remember, what has stayed with me all these years, is pulling the rebbe's beard and feeling comfortable in the lap of such a formidable person. When I read Martin Buber's *I and Thou* for the first time years later, I had some difficulty visualizing the intimacy of the I/thou relationship. Then, remembering how the rebbe had established such a close and immediate rapport with such a small boy, I understood Buber.

Cheder was not my only school. Some of my most enduring lessons were learned either in the community or in the family. As a little boy, I was eager to run errands for Mother. These were not only mitzvohs (good deeds) but also sources of delight, for I enjoyed helping her. Each request of hers seemed to enhance the special love I had for her, and she for me. Yet it was a love no more special, of course, than that she shared with her other children. Late one Friday afternoon, when I was seven or eight, my mother asked me to run an urgent errand.

She had suddenly discovered that we did not have proper Sabbath candles. She gave me money to go to the store and buy the four candles we needed. When I got there, I saw some chocolate-covered cookies. They looked so delicious that I wanted them very much, but I had money for only four candles. Or, I suddenly thought, I had money for two candles and two cookies. Yielding to temptation, I bought two candles and two cookies and ate the cookies as soon as I left the store.

When I got home, I placed the two new candles in two of the candlesticks. The four candles—two new and two old—didn't look right. I removed the candlesticks with the old candles from the table. Still not right. I then took the two new candles in their candlesticks to the mantel over the fireplace, in front of a mirror. That is where I placed the Sabbath candles. When Mother came in to set the table for the Sabbath meal, she asked why there were not four candles and four candlesticks. I said that there were: I took her over to the mantel, pointed to the two candlesticks and the mirror, and said, "Look, there are the four candlesticks."

Mother looked hard at me but said nothing. I thought I would be punished severely, at least that I would be spanked. But Mother did nothing, nor did she say anything about it during the Sabbath meal. She said nothing the next morning, either, or at the noon meal. No one said anything about it, not Mother, not Father. Everyone behaved as if everything were perfectly normal. After the noon meal on the Sabbath, it was customary for my father to take a nap and for my mother to read religious literature while we children went outside to play. In the middle of the afternoon we generally came inside for an afternoon snack, which had a special name, "Shabbos oibst" (Sabbath fruit). That afternoon at 3, we all gathered around the table as usual. Everyone else got an apple, plums, and cherries. But I received only half an apple instead of a whole one, one plum instead of two, and two cherries instead of four.

When I asked her why, she put the fruit in a bowl, took it to the mirror over the mantel, pointed, and said, "Here is the other half of your fruit."

"Haskel Traskalawski is violating the Sabbath publicly!"

The words filled our small *stiebel* (house of prayer) that Sabbath morning in the fall of my tenth year. In the door stood the shammes (beadle) of the *Beis Midrash,* the second-largest synagogue of Zdunska Wola. He stared first at our rebbe, then at my father and Reb Mendel, then at me and all the other boys and men. Crowded behind him, like schoolchildren trying to get into a circus, stood many of the worshippers from the Beis Midrash.

"Come," the shammes said to us, "the rabbi has said that we must prevent this desecration of the Sabbath from continuing."

So we put away our prayer books and joined the forty or so people from the Beis Midrash. All of us followed the shammes as he joined the rabbi and people from other shuls in the procession toward Szadekerstreet, where Haskel Traskalawski, kosher butcher and son-in-law of a kosher butcher, was working on a road crew, spreading gravel and pounding rocks with a stone-masher.

Until a month before, Haskel Traskalawski's modest butcher shop was in our *rathaus* (town hall). Its door faced the inner courtyard rather than the street. As a boy, I played through much of the building and of course knew all the shopkeepers. I was afraid of Haskel Traskalawski without knowing why, for he never did anything to me. He was burly and clean-shaven, with the huge forearms of someone who lifted heavy objects for a living. And he was not a Hasid, as we were.

On the way to Szadekerstreet, we discussed Haskel Traskalawski's serious affront to Jewish law. Three months before, a desperately poor woman had approached him in his butcher shop late one Friday afternoon.

"Haskel," she told him. "We have had a hard week. There's no meat for the Sabbath meal. Do you have any meat left over that I could buy for just a few coins?"

Haskel and her husband were friends, and on the spur of the moment he nodded yes and reached under the counter for a cut of beef normally reserved for gentiles, for it contained the sinew from the hollow of the thigh where it meets the hip socket. That cut, coming from that part of the thigh where Jacob was wounded as he wrestled with the angel, is not to be eaten by the Children of Israel. Although Haskel identified the cut to her, he also said that the animal had been slaughtered in the proper kosher manner. Did she still want the meat, even though it was from the lower part of the animal? She said yes.

That evening, the woman boasted about her bargain to her husband. He repeated the story to a friend, who told it to someone else, until at last, distorted by endless repetition, the story had Haskel Traskalawski accused, tried, and convicted in the court of gossip as a kosher butcher who sold nonkosher meat to Jews. It was as serious a scandal as I remember in Zdunska Wola. The matter was brought before the leaders of the community. They, with the consent of Haskel Traskalawski's own rabbi from the Beis Midrash, revoked his license as a kosher butcher. Although he was allowed to continue to sell nonkosher meat, his business soon dried up and he had to close the shop. After looking in vain for work within the Jewish community, he finally turned to the Polish Socialist Party for help and within a few days was offered a job on the road crew of a Polish construction company. All Polish construction companies worked six days a week, and that included Saturday. Faced with that dilemma during his very first week on the job, Haskel Traskalawski must have decided that in order not to be fired he had to violate the Sabbath.

On the first Sabbath that Haskel joined the labor brigade, most of the Jews of Zdunska Wola were as usual in their *stieblach* (houses of prayer). In the Beis Midrash, just before the Torah was to be read, a woman whom I only knew of as Reilla came through the door and announced to all assembled that she had a matter of great urgency to discuss. By law and by custom, the Torah reading could be stopped in this way, but to do so without sufficient cause was a serious offense, for this forum was like a court of last resort. At first the congregation was more amused than surprised, for Reilla was known to be unbalanced. The children of our shtetl used to trail after her in the street, calling her names and taunting her. Now, in a voice shaking with rage, she accused the congregation in general and its rabbi in particular of turning their backs on a fellow Jew.

"You did the wrong thing in taking away Haskel Traskalawski's kosher license," she said, "for you took away his means of earning of a living. And what is he doing right now while you are

all here reading the Torah? He is out there on Szadekerstreet working with a Polish road crew."

A stunned silence greeted this accusation, for everyone knew
the issues involved. If the community had destroyed Haskel's
means of earning a living, then the community was guilty. If in
addition Haskel was violating the Sabbath as a result, then the
entire community was violating the Sabbath.

"I will not let you read the Torah unless you do something
about it," Reilla continued, looking at the women in the gallery
for moral support. But they only stared back at her in shock.

"Reilla is right," the rabbi said. "I am going right now to
Szadekerstreet to see if we can't persuade Haskel to give up his
job." With Reilla and the men of the congregation following him,
the rabbi left the building, collected us at our stiebel, for we were
on the way, and marched to Haskel's work place.

Haskel's working companions, large, heavily-muscled Poles,
put down their shovels and pickaxes and gawked at this odd and
unprecedented parade approaching them, led by the rabbi in his
tallis. They laughed and jeered, but the rabbi ignored them.

Going up to Haskel, he said, "It is good that you have found a
job, Haskel, but to work on the Sabbath? Is this the way for a responsible Jew to behave?"

Haskel was not intimidated. "Is it responsible for a man to let
his wife and children starve? A butcher I am no longer. I can't
even buy a loaf of bread. What can I do? Become a sales clerk? No
one wanted to hire me. Become a street sweeper? It doesn't pay.
This job pays enough."

"We are a community," the rabbi responded. "We'll do something."

"For two months you could have done something," Haskel
said, wiping the sweat from his face. "So why did you wait till
now? I have had almost no income for two months. The porter
work I sometimes got was not enough. I am already in violation

of the Sabbath, and I will continue to violate it. I need the job. I need to feed my family. I will stay with this company."

The Poles applauded. The foreman separated himself from them and walked toward the rabbi. "You have heard what Mr. Traskalawski said. Please leave now. We have to get back to work."

The rabbi looked at Haskel a long time, then turned away, defeated.

"Wait!" The voice belonged to Dovid Najdat, one of the leading merchants in town. "Haskel, I can find something for you to do at my store. You could at least work as a porter for me."

"And what will you pay?" asked Haskel.

"Do you want me to negotiate on the Sabbath?" responded Dovid. "You know that I can't do that. But I can promise you that it will be a fair wage. We can come to an understanding tomorrow, and the rabbi can be present for the discussion."

The rabbi of the Beis Midrash nodded his agreement. Haskel gazed at his Polish co-workers and then at all of us. After what seemed like an eternal silence, he put down his tools, shook hands with his foreman and co-workers, and then walked back with us to the Beis Midrash synagogue. When we entered, the women in the gallery burst into applause. We all stayed for the rest of the service. At the very end, the rabbi spoke words that I have never forgotten: "The day began with the desecration of God's name, and if it were not for the faith and courage of one woman, it might have ended like that. But Reilla was brave enough to interrupt the service and to bring this matter to our attention. She reminded us of the grave sin which inadvertently we all committed by not looking to the need of one of our own. If the sin had continued, we would all have been tainted. There is no greater mitzvah than to help a neighbor and a fellow Jew in need."

Although I knew from my teachers that anyone with a major grievance had the authority to stop the congregation from reading the Torah, I had never known of it being done in my home-town. And although I knew of the obligation we had to help a fellow Jew in need, I had never witnessed such collective action before. That experience helped me appreciate the ethical and practical complexities of Judaism in our community, but it was my father who taught me what Haskel Traskalawski's actions really meant.

"In the end," Father commented as we walked home, "what persuaded Haskel was *dos pintele Yid,* that small spark of Judaism in the hidden chambers of the heart of every Jew. People forget about it or think that it has gone but suddenly, especially at times of crisis, it surfaces and reminds them who they are. When Haskel saw that he was facing the choice of living as an observant Jew or not, it was dos pintele Yid that spoke to him. That spark is in all of us, Itsekel, and it is indestructible."

I am sometimes asked if, as a boy growing up in Zdunska Wola, I could sense dark clouds on the horizon. The truth is, I could not. Although my hometown was not paradise, there was mostly peace among Jews, ethnic Germans, and Poles. I don't remember much overt anti-Semitism on the main streets of town. That occurred only in gentile neighborhoods, where, if you were careless enough to wander onto those streets, you could be hit with a stone or could hear insults. We were used to that and did not consider it noteworthy.

Things began to change, however, after Hitler became chancellor of Germany in 1933. A barrage of anti-Semitic propaganda began in our nationalist press, especially in a newspaper called *Oredownik,* the main organ of the Endecja (National Democrats), a viciously anti-Semitic political party. Its viciousness caused much concern in our community, as in all the Jewish communities in Poland, but I remember the Polish and German leaders of the town reassuring us that nothing could possibly happen in Zdunska Wola. "Our people live and work together," they said. "Why should things be disturbed? No one would benefit from that."

Then one spring day in 1936, two weeks before Passover and Easter, three Christian boys disappeared. The sons of a butcher, a shoemaker, and a baker, they had been playing in the dunes at the edge of a beautiful pine forest about five kilometers from town. The dunes were ideal places to play, for the hills were large and there was a summer resort nearby. Rumors of unrest and of anti-Semitic riots in other parts of Poland had already reached my hometown before the boys disappeared. There were even rumors that we were being accused again—as we had been in former centuries—of sacrificing gentile children for our Passover celebrations. After the boys disappeared, our community feared the possibility of a pogrom, and our young Jewish men began training in self-defense. Suddenly there were many meetings and activities, but I didn't go to them because, at thirteen, I was still too young for such things. The *Oredownik* blamed the Jewish community for the boys' disappearance. It intensified its call for a boycott of Jewish stores and for limiting further Jewish access to trades, professions, and universities. Tensions ran high. We heard news of pogroms in other parts of Poland. Father was especially worried because our store, which sold shoemaking materials and notions, was in the town hall and thus might be targeted first in any attack.

During these anxious days Boleslaw Marczyniak entered our store one afternoon, just before closing. I was in the anteroom, and Father was at the store register. Mr. Marczyniak had been one of our favorite customers for years. He always paid his bills on time, and my father in turn had made a practice of giving him the best merchandise at the best price. Gradually he and Father had become close business friends. Although they never talked about their friendship, they had great affection for each other. Mr.

Marczyniak first apologized for coming so late in the afternoon. Then he said he had done so on purpose because he wanted to talk to my father in private after business hours. He was a former noncommissioned officer in the Polish cavalry, he continued, and knew that all the wild rumors in the air worried Father.

I have never forgotten what he said then: "Rest assured, Mr. Najman," he said, calling my father by the surname we had before the Germans converted it to Neuman in the camps, "if anything happens, I will be here instantly in my uniform, with all my medals and with my carbine. I will defend you and your store from any attack."

In the anteroom and out of Mr. Marczyniak's sight, I thought of a talmudic saying: "The righteous of all nations have a share in the world to come." After Mr. Marczyniak had left, I asked my father if he were one of those righteous men.

"Yes, indeed," he replied. "Of that there can be no doubt." I felt comforted that we knew such a decent human being, one willing to put his life on the line for a Jewish friend.

A week later the three boys were found. In their games among the sand dunes, they had been building tunnels for sand castles. All three were in the tunnels when the sand—which had become heavy with spring rains during a general thaw—collapsed on them. An official investigation was launched. At its end, the head of the police declared in a public statement that it had all been but a tragic accident, that it could have happened anywhere, and that no one was to blame. Although the *Oredownik* also agreed that it had been an accident, it never apologized for having accused the Jewish community of foul play. Rather, the newspaper stridently demanded that the government provide funds for a supervised playground and that its own sponsored youth organization be designated as the official supervisor. There was no pogrom in Zdunska Wola that spring, but there was one in the town of Przytek in the region of Lublin.

Two or three weeks after the investigation was closed, Mr. Marczyniak came by the store with his carbine, dressed in his cavalry officer's uniform and resplendent in all his medals, just to show us how he would have looked defending us and our property. His friendship with my father deepened. Mr. Marczyniak remained a good customer and friend and continued to come to the store even after the Germans occupied Zdunska Wola. Then the Germans closed the store in the summer of 1940. They established the ghetto in early fall. Contacts between gentiles and Jews were forbidden. We never saw Mr. Marczyniak again after that. It was rumored that he joined a Polish underground group operating out of the forests in eastern Poland.

TWO

Reb Mendel

My religious education began at age three with Reb Arele. It continued in local cheders until 1934. That September Father sent me to the yeshiva in Kalisz. In August of 1935 I returned to Zdunska Wola for a year a half. Although I would also later study at the Rebbe's Court in Zgierz in the spring of 1937 and at the prestigious Emek-halacha Yeshiva in Warsaw from September 1938 until August of 1939, it was during my eighteen months back home in 1935 and 1936 that I learned the most. It was then that I would study with a profound and wise teacher.

In 1935 I had complained to my parents that I didn't like the yeshiva in Kalisz, that it wasn't rigorous enough, that I wasn't making friends, and that my teachers weren't interesting enough. But the truth is that I was homesick. I missed my mother and father, my two brothers and six sisters. Although my father wanted me to study in a major yeshiva, my mother encouraged me always to study in Zdunska Wola. For her, my being at home was as important as my studying in the renowned Yeshiva of Kalisz. So I came home, where I was at loose ends for a while until I began going regularly to the stiebel to pray and study with other men and boys.

In Kalisz I had discovered a Jewish bookstore, which, in addition to carrying the usual religious literature, also had pamphlets for sale under the counter. These pamphlets—serialized novels, really—contained what were then viewed as lurid stories and had provocative pictures of women on the covers. It was not the sort of reading for a pious yeshiva boy, but to a teenager in the flush of adolescence the pamphlets were irresistible. I bought a few and packed them inside my coat in my suitcase before returning to Zdunska Wola.

As I prepared to pray in the stiebel a few days after my return, I loosened the *gartel* (prayer rope) around my waist and released my left arm from the jacket sleeve. One of the pamphlets—and I still remember the low-cut blouse of the woman on the cover—fell out of the sleeve and onto the stiebel floor. Immediately Zalmen, a pudgy former classmate in the cheders and always jealous of me, picked it up and ran around, showing it to everyone and crying out, "Look at what Isaac is reading! Look at what Isaac is reading!"

It was a moment of total humiliation. I felt that no one would want to have me as a study partner after that and that no teacher would consent to teach me. Indeed, for two days my father and other men in the stiebel talked about what should be done. I despaired of my lost reputation.

In the midst of all the talk, Mordcha Mendel Strykowski approached Father and offered to become my permanent teacher. Gratefully, he accepted, and I became the student of the man who was to be my greatest and most beloved teacher. From that moment on my indiscretion was forgotten, for no one believed that Reb Mendel would teach Torah to a boy who was unworthy. After his first meeting with me, Reb Mendel never mentioned the incident of the pamphlet. Ashamed that my behavior had prompted him to volunteer to teach me and anxious to succeed in his eyes, I tried to live up to his trust and kindness. I became Reb Mendel's disciple.

Reb Mendel was in his mid-fifties, stocky and vigorous, with a thick, graying beard and bushy eyebrows. He was so swarthy that everyone called him "der schwarze" (swarthy) Mordcha Mendel. His warm, open, brown eyes could upon occasion seem so luminous that they would penetrate your soul. Although he often seemed lost in contemplation, he was well informed about world affairs as well as about politics on both the local and national level. He was not, however, a good businessman. Even though he had many customers in his small grocery store, and even though the store was in a prime location, he never seemed to have enough money. People speculated that he gave too much away. Some said that certain peasants stole him blind, coming to the store in large numbers in order to distract him while one or two shoplifted. Whatever the case, making money didn't seem to matter to him. For him, the purpose of life was the study of Torah.

Reb Mendel spoke always in calm and measured tones. Behind every word we sensed a deep spirituality, the wisdom that comes from both experience and reflection. By the time he became my teacher, he was legendary. We felt that his serene wisdom had something to do with his wartime experience and how it had come to enrich his study of Torah. He had been in the German army during World War I and toward its end was taken prisoner in Russia and sent to Siberia. For four years his family heard nothing of him. Then, one day in early 1922, a shabbily dressed stranger, bearded and thin, arrived in Zdunska Wola and entered Reb Mendel's store. A seven-year-old girl stood behind the cash register. The stranger greeted the little girl. She looked at the poor starving Jew and immediately took some change from the cash register to offer him. The stranger began to cry. Thinking she had not given him enough, she dug out some more change and offered that. When he did not leave, she called to her mother in the back room to bring the stranger some food. Her mother looked at the stranger and screamed. It was her husband, Reb Mendel. All of them cried and embraced. What had kept him alive as a prisoner, he told them, was the hope of seeing his family again and seeing how his daughter was being taught things of the spirit. He had cried at first, he told his daughter, because she had learned the mitzvah of *tsedakah* (charitable giving) so well. Her mother had taught her well in his absence; her compassion made his own suffering worthwhile.

And so Reb Mendel resumed his former life, rising at 5 to study Torah in the stiebel until 8:30 or 9 in the morning, spending the rest of the day at the store, and returning to the stiebel or his family in the evenings. Although he did not look for disciples, young men sought him out for advice and guidance in study.

When the railroad finally came to Zdunska Wola, the town council decided to dedicate the station with a public ceremony, and many Hasidim went to see the wonder that would unite us to the rest of Poland and the world. Reb Mendel also went, accompanied by some younger Hasidic students. They all listened to the station master and politicians make speeches about the modern world and progress. Afterward, as Reb Mendel and the young men walked home, they asked, "What does the train mean?"

"What does the train mean?" he mused. "Let me tell you what a Hasidic rebbe said. The steam engine teaches us that if one is hot, he can pull many cold ones behind him. So, too, fervor and intensity in spiritual matters may pull along those who are less intense. A train comes in and leaves at the exact time. That means that if you are just one minute late you may miss everything. If you are late in the study of Torah, you may miss the holy one, blessed be he. And with the train we are linked to the rest of Europe."

"And what is so important about being linked to Europe?" they asked him.

"All linkages help to unify a shattered world," he answered. "Telephones are also such linkages, for the telephone teaches us that what is said here can be heard over there, whether over the wires or through prayer. We are linked by the telegraph, too, which teaches us that every word counts and must be paid for."

Although I did not hear Reb Mendel's comments firsthand (he made the remarks in 1922, the year in which I was born), I heard him say many similar things as my teacher. My first meeting with him as a student was typical of our exchanges, for it contained both a spiritual lesson and a matter-of-fact statement about the difficulties ahead. The first thing he asked was how I was feeling. I said that I was afraid I had ruined my life and was beginning to comment on the incident with Zalmen and the pamphlet when he gently interrupted.

"Nu, Isaac," he said. "Remember what Reb Nachman of Braslav used to say: 'The whole world is but a narrow bridge, and the main thing is not to be afraid.'"

He smiled and paused, letting the silence build as if he expected an answer. When I said nothing, for I was trying to absorb the statement and apply it to my shame, he resumed, "If you want to study Torah with me, you must be here at five each morning, for I get up at five and come to the stiebel. Are you willing to do that?"

"Yes, of course," I answered. "And I will light the stove each day."

"We will begin tomorrow," he said. "Do you have any particular tractate in mind?"

"No."

"Then we will begin at the beginning," he said, "with the first tractate of Berachot (Blessings)."

So I began to study with Reb Mendel. I soon learned that it was not enough just to read a text. One had to bring it to life by devoting one's entire mind and heart to it, as if it were being spoken right then and there by the old masters, who themselves were testing our understanding and the quality of our attention. I learned from Reb Mendel that to be a student of Torah one had to prepare oneself as if for a special and dangerous mission. Perhaps it was his experience as a soldier that taught him the importance of fulfilling a mission with all of one's heart and mind. Although my mission might be special, Reb Mendel taught me, it was no more important than that of any other person. As a Jew, I was to prepare for the coming of the Messiah, for redemption. To do that, it was necessary to endow every part of my life with spirituality. Mundane things were to become as holy as the study of Torah. If we should fall, we should then get up again and work at our task, for the holy one, blessed be he, was waiting for us to succeed. Although no one Jew could accomplish redemption individually, every Jew had to be like a soldier in a battalion and do their duty.

From the moment we discussed the first Mishnah of Berachot, I felt fortunate that Zalmen had humiliated me that day in the stiebel, because it moved Reb Mendel to become my teacher. I had studied Berachot before, of course, but I had not heard it interpreted the way Reb Mendel did for me on that very first morning.

"When is the appropriate time," the tractate asks, "to recite the morning prayers of the Shema?" "The appropriate time," goes the answer, "is when you can recognize a fellow human being."

"What is the meaning of this?" Reb Mendel asked. "What does it mean 'to recognize a fellow human being?'"

"It indicates the time of day," I answered, "when we can see someone's face and distinguish it from other objects."

"That is incomplete," he said. "Try again."

I don't remember what else I said, but each time the answer was not quite sufficient. Finally, Reb Mendel said that to recognize other persons was to see in them the image of the divine. Thus, the appropriate time to pray was upon such a realization—and that could be always. It was only on the surface that this text had to do with the time of day; on a deeper level it had to do with spirituality, insight, and seeing the divine.

I thus began to learn to go beyond the literal meaning of the text and reach for an understanding that was deeper and more spiritual than any I had ever tried to attain. Reb Mendel taught me to pay attention to the small details of life. He taught me that no task, however menial, was without a spiritual foundation if done with devotion and awareness. Once I wondered whether for a while it could be someone else's responsibility to light the oven in the stiebel at five in the morning. Reb Mendel explained that I was lighting the flame of spirituality every morning and should consider making the fire to be the same as making a prayer. Both start with a single point of light and heat, and soon both spread to all the coals and all the limbs. Begin a prayer from the flame in your heart and soon, as the Psalmist says, "All your bones shall speak." Everything, Reb Mendel added, has both a practical and a spiritual aspect. It is important from a practical perspective to light a fire properly so a flame rises. If the flame is horizontal, the room will fill with smoke. Showing me how to place the coals and light them so the flame would rise, he added that a prayer, like the flame of a well-constructed fire, should also rise.

As important as it was to study Torah, it was equally important, thought Reb Mendel, to live in harmony with your community. The petty fights that occurred in our town troubled him deeply. He saw these fights as splintering further an already splintered world in which only three of the ten emanations of the divine remained. The other seven were scattered, adding to the brokenness of the world. Reb Mendel became a peacemaker, healing rifts in families and among friends, settling disputes among business associates, and reconciling enemies. Many such fights were caused, he said, by each side thinking itself more deserving and moral than the other side.

He likened the fights to the story of the two siblings who lived just after the destruction of the Second Temple: It happened that the son and daughter of Rabbi Ishmael Ben Elisha were taken captive and sold to two different masters. The two children were both teenagers, about a year apart in age, both talented, both strong and healthy, and both physically attractive. They served their respective masters well, were gradually given increased responsibilities in the households, and in time came to be considered indispensable, each one a jewel in the master's crown. After some time, the masters happened to meet and, not knowing they were speaking about brother and sister, began to brag about their slaves.

"Mine," said the one about the girl, "is intelligent and beautiful and gracious, with a singing voice like an angel, with eyes so blue that they put the sky to shame, and with manners so gentle that they caress even the most hardened soldier."

"Mine," answered the other about the boy, "is handsome and strong. He is good with horses. He knows languages and is so good with words that he can make anyone believe that black is white."

Back and forth the boasting went, each master smugly confident of the superiority of his slave. Finally they became so impressed by the reputed quality of both slaves that they decided to mate the slaves to one another and share in the offspring. They put the boy and girl in a darkened room and shut the door. The boy went to one corner and the girl to another.

He said to himself, "I am the son of high priests. How is it that I should marry a slave girl?"

She said to herself, "I am the daughter of high priests. How is it that I should be commanded to marry a slave?"

They cried all night, each in their own corner. When the morning light came, each waited for the light to strike the other's face in order to begin the morning prayer. The moment that the sun shone on their faces, they recognized each other, embraced, and wept. "What fools we were," they lamented, "to have wasted the entire night in tears and in being apart." When the two masters opened the door a short time later, they found that the slaves were actually brother and sister.

"What does this story teach us?" asked Reb Mendel. "As long as we are in the darkness of both ignorance and exile, we don't know who the other is. But only with the coming of the light and of the sun can we begin to see the truth. Much pain in the world can be avoided," he continued after a long and meditative pause, "if we base our actions on knowledge rather than on ignorance, if we are motivated by humility rather than by arrogance, and if we recognize the divine in other human beings."

"Don't you see?" I heard him once say to Abraham Ozorowicz, the son-in-law with whom he frequently studied Torah, "don't you see that it is Satan that is causing these cleavages in the heart, that it is Satan who wants us to be ignorant and arrogant and conceited? So much hatred in the world is causeless." When he said this, the pain in his face made me wonder if Reb Mendel were one of the thirty-six righteous men who are placed in the world to bear its suffering and understand pain.

From another conversation with Abraham Ozorowicz, Reb Mendel illustrated the theme of causeless hatred. He told of a rich merchant of his grandfather's generation who gave an elaborate dinner party. The merchant sent his servant all over town with invitations for the crème de la crème. By mistake, the servant gave an invitation to a peddler. Instead of making the best of the situation, the merchant first humiliated the peddler in front of the other guests by ordering him to leave. When that didn't work, he offered him money. Finally, he had his servants throw the peddler out. By the end of the evening, the rich man's heart was full of hatred for the peddler, who had come to the party in all innocence. Through no fault of his own, he had disturbed the rich merchant's sense of his own importance. That was unforgivable. For the rest of their lives they remained enemies, unable to break free of the part in which the playwright Satan had cast them: the merchant hating, the peddler hated.

"What the merchant and the peddler needed," said Reb Mendel, "was a good rebbe who could help them break out of the cage of ill will in which they found themselves trapped. Often it is only a small thing that starts us on our downward spiral. Just as often, all we need to avoid destruction is a little kindness, a little bit of good to counteract the seed of evil that has been sown. Such a seed will not germinate in the soil of kindness."

Although Reb Mendel did not relate this explanation to my humiliation at Zalmen's hands, I understood that it described my situation and explained why Reb Mendel had chosen to become my teacher.

I heard many such stories during my time with Reb Mendel, and although many of them were familiar, his angle on them brought them to life and made them more profound than I had thought. One, which appears in the Talmud, addresses the question of how to pray when traveling:

> Rabbi Yossi says, "Once, when I was traveling, I entered one of the ruins of Jerusalem at the side of the road in order to pray. Elijah, may he be remembered for good, arrived and waited for me outside. When I finished my prayer, I came out to the road again and ran into him. Elijah said to me, 'Peace to you, master.' I returned the greeting. Then he asked, 'My son, why did you enter a ruin?'"
>
> "I entered in order to pray," I replied.
>
> "You should have prayed on the road," he responded.
>
> "I would have, but I was afraid of other travelers or bandits."
>
> "And what did you hear inside the ruin?" Elijah asked.
>
> "I heard a voice that was cooing like a dove, saying, 'Woe unto me that I exiled my children, destroyed my city and burned my altar.'"
>
> "My son," answered Elijah. "I swear to you. Not only does that voice echo during this very hour, but it echoes any time that the children of Israel enter the Beis Midrash and say 'Amein, may the great name be blessed.' God himself shakes his head and says, 'Happy is the king who is so praised. And woe unto the children who were driven from their father's table.'"

Reb Mendel commented:

> The Talmud says that we learn three things from this encounter: that we do not enter a ruin, that if we pray while traveling our prayer should be short, and that we may pray while on a journey. But now we see something more interesting. In the text itself the question is raised, "Why is it forbidden to enter a ruin?" Several answers are given. The first is that the ruin may be dangerous and could collapse while you are praying. The second is that entering a ruin might arouse suspicion. People could suspect you of plotting against the government or believe that you are meeting a harlot in secret. One shouldn't take unnecessary risks while traveling, and it is a definite risk to enter a ruin.
>
> But I think that there is more to this story. It also teaches that when you stand at the ruin of your life or of your culture, your prayer should be short in order to be effective. It is not the length of the prayer or its eloquence that counts, but rather its intensity. It is not how many pages of the prayer book you go through, but how many pages of the prayer book go through you.

One morning at five, I came into the stiebel as usual. After lighting the stove, I took a volume from the shelf to my right and opened it to the page we had been studying the morning before. But my mind wasn't on the text in that well-worn folio. Two days before I had gotten into a fight with Zalmen. We had argued, and in the heat of anger I had called him names. Now Zalmen was avoiding me. The situation bothered me so much that I wanted to ask Reb Mendel about it. At half-past five he came in. He washed his hands, reciting a prayer for that, and dried them on the roller. Then he sat down on the long bench at the table in front of me, folded his hands, and looked at me quietly. After a minute he said, "Nu?" Sometimes we would start like that, sometimes we would begin with a text he would ask me to read. If he sensed that I had something on my mind, he would simply say, "Nu?" and pause, allowing the silence to fill the space between us.

"Have you had this problem before, Isaac?" asked Reb Mendel, after I had told him of my fight with Zalmen.

"Yes, Reb Mendel," I answered. "Two or three times, but with other boys."

"Ah," said Reb Mendel. "The Talmud is not silent on that problem." As he gathered himself to speak in his slow, measured way, I sensed, as I often did, the great talmudic masters standing behind him and on both sides of me, looking on and stroking their beards. Even though many of the great masters had been olive-skinned Mediterraneans, I did not see them as Sefardim. I saw ruddy-faced men dressed in the heavy Central European *pelz-mantel* (fur coats) of winter, with round fur hats. Reb Mendel settled into his story:

> The king had just completed his beautiful palace on which he had worked for many years. He was very happy with the finished work, and since many of the townspeople had been curious and solicitous about all the renovations, he decided to open the palace for a day to all the town. Everyone came. Most people wandered about the palace complimenting this or that touch. Three of the king's visitors, however, did not seem to be impressed.
>
> "If the beams were not so visible, it would all be nicer," said one.
>
> "If the columns were larger, the aesthetic effect would be more powerful," said the second.
>
> "If there were more windows," said the third, "then there would be more light in the rooms and we could see more clearly."
>
> The king's advisor, who had been listening to these three ungracious men as they wandered through the palace, finally decided to confront them.
>
> To the first he said, "Wouldn't it be better if you had three noses? Then you could smell better."
>
> To the second he said, "Wouldn't it be better if you had three ears? Then you could hear better."
>
> To the third he said, "Wouldn't it be better if you had three eyes, especially if you had one of them in the back of your head? Then you could see better."

The three men understood what they had done and, ashamed, quietly left the palace and returned to their homes.

"Does this story mean," I asked, "that you shouldn't criticize someone who has just finished an important task?"

"Yes," said Reb Mendel, "but it means more than that."

"That we shouldn't criticize people if our criticism comes from ignorance or jealousy?"

"Also yes," said Reb Mendel, "but it is deeper than that. Think about the noses, the ears, and eyes." Seeing that I was silent, he finished softly. "All of us have two ears, two nostrils, and two eyes. We need them in order to hear, to smell, and to see. But we have only one mouth. That means that we should take more in than we give out. We should listen more than we talk. Silence is better than speech. It is possible to say too much, to say things in anger or passion that we wish later we had not said and that we would not have said if only we had remembered that we had two ears but only one mouth."

It was typical of Reb Mendel not to criticize me directly. He was fascinated by the larger questions of character and integrity and less interested in orchestrating individual events. He never told me specifically what to do. I don't remember how Zalmen and I made up after that particular fight, but I do remember that for several months thereafter I was quieter than I had been and got into fewer fights. I began to learn how to keep my mouth shut.

Around 8:30, after our time together, Reb Mendel would usually either pray quietly by himself or with a minyan before going to his store. On Mondays and Thursdays, when the Torah would be read at the morning services, there would often be more people in the stiebel, and I looked forward especially to the *jahrzeiten* (anniversaries of someone's death), for that person's relatives would bring a bit of cake and other refreshments as well as a small bottle of vodka. We would all receive a bit of vodka, recite the blessing, say "Le chaim," and remember a departed one.

On mornings after a new moon it would be even more festive. We called this *Rosh Chodesh* (new moon), and we would not only eat special food but would also sing special songs in honor of the moon. On one such occasion I became curious.

"Why?" I asked Reb Mendel, "do we make such a fuss about the moon and none about the sun?"

"First," he replied, "you know of course that pagan worshippers considered the sun a deity. And since we separate ourselves from pagan worshippers, we don't want to worship what they worship. Second, the moon never stands still. It is always changing, either waxing or waning, growing or dying, like all human beings, like all life. And so we celebrate its birth as we celebrate the birth of human beings. We are glad to see them come into the world."

"But there is more," Reb Mendel added, and looked at his hands, resting quietly as always on the table before him. His voice took on a meditative, distant tone. "In the beginning, both the sun and the moon were equally radiant. They shone with equal power. The moon did not like this equivalency in rank and complained to God. 'How can two kings,' she said to God, 'use one and the same crown? Shouldn't one king be superior to the other and have a larger crown?' 'You are quite right,' God replied. 'So while the sun will retain his radiance and his crown, you will have less radiance and will wear a smaller crown.'"

"So the moon is being punished?" I asked.

"In a way," answered Reb Mendel.

"And when will this punishment end?"

"It will only end when the world is finally redeemed and everything is returned to its former glory. Then, and not before, the moon will regain her radiance. Meanwhile, as long as the Jewish people and the world are not redeemed, the moon suffers along with us."

This was not the story I expected to hear about the origin of a festival, but by now I had come to expect the unexpected from Reb Mendel.

I would meet Reb Mendel not only in the mornings but sometimes also in the evenings, and then in the company of Father and other men. I was the only boy at these gatherings, and, I later came to learn, it was like listening to a panel of scholars at a conference or to professors in a seminar. During the warmer months, several of the men would often come to the stiebel in the evening and sit in the courtyard around the well, discussing the events of the day. Reb Mendel would be there, as would Uren Leib, a brilliant but embittered Cabalist who made his living as a peddler. Abraham Ozorowicz would sometimes accompany his father-in-law Reb Mendel. Avrum Yiedel Hirschberg, a gentle and quietly devout man who owned a restaurant and was Reb Mendel's best friend, would often come. My father began taking me to those courtyard sessions in the spring of 1936. Usually the discussions focused on national and international events. I am astonished when I now recall how prescient and penetrating their comments and analyses were. Of course, no one imagined how horrible and tragic the future was to be for all of us, but some of the men, natural skeptics like Uren Leib or soldiers like Reb Mendel, saw darkness ahead.

One evening, as we were discussing the Zionist dreams of the formation of a Jewish state in Palestine, Uren Leib quoted Talmud: "Aysi vlo echzei (Let him [the Messiah] come, but I don't want to see it)."

Although Reb Mendel was not as deeply pessimistic as Uren Leib and in no way could he be considered a bitter man, he nodded agreement.

"What does this mean?" I asked Reb Mendel later. "Why does Uren Leib not want to see the Messiah?"

"Because Uren Leib knows," said Reb Mendel, "that the time before the coming of the Messiah is known as *chevley leidah* (birth pangs). This will be a time of enormous pain and suffering, so much suffering that Uren Leib would rather not see the Messiah if in order to do so he would have to go through that suffering or see the world go through it. Before the coming of the Messiah there will be a war like that of Gog and Magog. Some of us believe that Zionists are forcing the hand of God by trying to create the Jewish state before the coming of the Messiah."

"Do you want to see the Messiah," I asked Reb Mendel, "if you know that before you do you must see the world in such pain?"

"I don't know, Isaac. I don't know."

That night, as Father and I walked home, we wondered what was going to happen. We wondered why Reb Mendel and Uren Leib saw such darkness, and we wondered what they saw.

I studied with Reb Mendel for more than eighteen months. Then, in the spring of 1937, I was sent to a yeshiva at the Rebbe's Court in Zgierz. I did not write to Reb Mendel and he did not write me, but I did not lose contact with him. My father would always say in his letters that Reb Mendel had asked for news about me, that he wished me well, and that he reminded me to study Torah with diligence. Although I had planned to continue studying in Zgierz, an illness forced me to return to Zdunska Wola in August of 1937, and for the next year I lived at home. During that year I did not study formally with Reb Mendel, and I came to miss those early mornings in the stiebel, the warmth of the stove, and the depth and compassion of my teacher's insights. We continued to have discussions, of course, just the two of us, and I continued to go with Father to the stiebel courtyard on warm evenings. Whenever I faced a choice in those days, no matter how trivial, I would wonder how Reb Mendel would decide and what he would say about my words or my actions.

In fall 1938 my father sent me to study at the acclaimed Emekhalacha Yeshiva in Warsaw. Although I had good teachers there, Reb Mendel remained my most influential one and the most beloved, and I thought of him constantly. Toward the end of August 1939 I came home for the summer break, intending to return to Warsaw after the holidays. I saw Reb Mendel only once or twice before September 1, the day the Germans invaded Poland and bombed my hometown. On September 3 my family and I tried to flee Zdunska Wola. We got as far as Zgierz, the town where our Hasidic rebbe lived, about sixty kilometers from Zdunska Wola. There we stopped to rest and get food.

Almost immediately, the German army came into town on motorcycles and in tanks. The army seemed to be everywhere. We had to decide whether to continue our escape route, and in which direction we should go, or turn back. I favored continuing along the eastward route toward Russia, but the way was long and dangerous, there were many of us in the family, and my sisters were very small. We didn't have enough food or money to last for such a journey. My mother and father decided that it would be best to go back to Zdunska Wola, where we had good neighbors and friends in all parts of town and where we thought we would be safer than on the open road, surrounded by the German army and many people as desperate as we were. Besides, we thought, the Germans would not stay long in our small town as an occupying force.

And so we returned. We entered Zdunska Wola again on September 10. Everything was changed, utterly changed. Glass covered the streets. Although not that much had happened to our apartment building beyond a number of broken windows, many other homes were in ruins and many factories burned. Father's store, like many others, had been completely emptied. Ghosts seemed to wander the streets, drifting through the ruins.

"Did you hear? Did you hear?" cried Uren Leib as he ran up to us in the street.

"Hear what?" my father asked.

"The world has been shattered again."

We thought he was referring to the glass on the street. "No," he said, in tears. "There is a cosmic tear in the heavens. The throne of glory has been shattered. Reb Mendel, Abraham Ozorowicz, and Avrum Yiedel Hirschberg have been shot. The Germans executed them."

Gradually we pieced the story together. After the war broke out and most of us decided to flee, Reb Mendel, Abraham Ozorowicz, and Avrum Yiedel Hirschberg chose to stay behind.

"There must be someone in town left," they told people who begged them to come with them, "to study Torah. It is especially important at these times that we continue to study Torah."

They went into the attic of Abraham Ozorowicz. There they stayed, in prayer and in study, and it was there that they were captured. People said later that an ethnic German had betrayed them, a simpleton of a man who used to wander around town singing "Ach, du lieber Augustin" and would do anything for a drink. The Germans must have promised him a drink if he could lead them to some Jewish hiding places.

A German officer and two soldiers came to Abraham Ozorowicz's attic. Surprised by Reb Mendel's wonderfully fluent German, the officer asked him in a conversational tone what he was doing there.

"Studying Talmud," said Reb Mendel.

"And what are you studying?"

"We are studying a passage that says, 'The righteous of all nations have a share of the world to come.'"

"That is a lie," the German officer snapped back. "That book doesn't have any such thing like that in it!"

"I swear," answered Reb Mendel, "on my word of honor as a former soldier of the German kaiser that I have not told a lie to you, an officer of the German army."

"Ihr Juden seid alle Schweinehunde (you Jews are all pigs)" the officer suddenly shouted and commanded that Reb Mendel,

Abraham Ozorowicz, and Avrum Yiedel Hirschberg be taken into custody for conspiracy against the German Reich. That evening several prominent ethnic Germans of Zdunska Wola went to the German commanding officer and pleaded on behalf of Reb Mendel and the other two men. Reb Mendel, they emphasized, was extraordinarily honest, kind, and decent. As one of the most respected citizens of the town, he would never engage in the subterfuge of which he was being accused.

"If the German army wants to accuse Jews of crimes," the ethnic Germans continued, "we can bring forward the names and addresses of several Jewish criminals in town who deserve to be captured and punished."

All this was to no avail. The next morning, Reb Mendel, Abraham Ozorowicz, and Avrum Yiedel Hirschberg were taken before a military tribunal and formally accused of conducting secret meetings against the orders of the German army and planning to overthrow the German Reich. The presiding SA officer, I was told, was a tall, thin man who never looked at the three accused men. He just read his notes and, denying the three a defense, sentenced them to death by firing squad as if he were delivering the weather report. That afternoon the Germans rounded up as many citizens as they could in such a short time and ordered them to the town square. When they had been assembled, the Germans brought Reb Mendel, Abraham Ozorowicz, and Avrum Yiedel Hirschberg; lined them up in front of the town hall; pronounced them enemies of the Reich; and shot them. The German army did it, Uren Leib told Father, in order to shock us all into submission.

We were horrified and numbed. For some time later all we talked about was how tragic and senselessly cruel the deaths had been. It was only after the war that I came to believe that what had seemed tragic to us then had turned out to be fortunate. Reb Mendel, Abraham Ozorowicz, and Avrum Yiedel Hirschberg did

THREE

The Gate of Tears

My mother's mother was engaged at twelve, married at fourteen, and widowed by thirty. By that time she had ten children, five sons and five daughters. My memory of her begins when she was more than forty, which is, of course, ancient to a five-year-old boy. I was struck then by the sweetness of her singing voice, the thickness of her body, and how her reading glasses deadened her face. To me, she was simply Grandma. To others, however, she was Widow Masha Tyger, proprietress and person of substance. She owned a store, an apartment building with nine small apartments, and one-eighth of Zdunska Wola's former town hall. This last was a one-story building of thick stone walls that had been converted to commercial use about the turn of the century. She had four spaces in the building, three of which she leased and kept the fourth for herself and my father.

There, in a store they shared, my father sold shoemaker's notions and leather goods, and she sold women's clothing and yard goods. The store had no name and no display window. It did not even have a sign on the door. "People know that we are here," Father once told me, going back to his Talmud, which he kept under the counter so he could read between customers. I had just asked for permission to put up a metal placard over the door to announce the presence of the store and its owners: "Tyger and Najman."

Neither he nor my grandmother had much interest in accumulating money, although she was better at making it than he was. Many people considered her to be an astute businesswoman, and she could have become prosperous. But in fact she did not. Her properties were heavily mortgaged, and she extended too many loans to too many customers whom she knew would have great difficulty repaying her. Also, in order to ensure good marriages for her daughters, she had to assemble substantial dowries.

By 1936, when my family moved into her building and into what would become our last apartment, Grandmother's furnishings in her own apartment in the same building echoed a more comfortable past, long since eroded. Now her furnishings might be considered faded Biedermeier, its solidity typical of many Central European homes in the late nineteenth century. I think of them more as *bekovid* (respectable). Of her four Sabbath candlesticks, two were silver and two were copper. She had two menorahs, both modest. A *mizrach* (decorated paper cut-out) indicated which wall in the apartment faced the East. On another wall hung a painting of the western wall in Jerusalem.

My most vivid memories before the age of eight are either of books or teachers. Opposite Grandmother's favorite sitting chair and small table was a low bookcase with glass doors, containing perhaps thirty books, all of them having to do with religion in one way or another. Most were written in both Hebrew and Yiddish. A multivolume *machzor* (prayer book) in both Hebrew and Yiddish contained the liturgy for each holiday. Of all her books, those she read the most were a slightly charred prayer book with psalms, the *Korban Mincha* (The Sacrifice of the Late Afternoon), which always lay on the table next to her chair and which she refused to replace, and a worn edition of the *Tsena U'rena,* a work intended for women. This work consists of the five books of Moses in Yiddish, with added stories and commentaries.

The *Korban Mincha* is at the center of my most dramatic early memory. One Sabbath afternoon when I was about five, a fire broke out at the town hall. At the time, although Grandmother had an apartment behind her store in that building, our family lived in an apartment on the opposite side of the town square. I wanted to go out on our balcony to see the fire but was afraid to do so. The balcony was forbidden territory, not because I might fall but because I might hear bad language from passersby in the street. From our main window, I watched the smoke, the tongues of flame, and the police pushing back the crowd. People went into our store and came out with goods, which they then put on the sidewalk in front of either Grandmother or Father.

I remember seeing the police physically restrain men who wanted to go back into the store but then suddenly drop their arms when someone I later knew as Puttermilch dashed in. The police were afraid of him, for he was physically the strongest Jew in town and also belonged to the Black Hand, Zdunska Wola's Jewish version of the Mafia. He was even rumored to be its ringleader. Thus, when Puttermilch ran into our store, everyone thought that he had done so to steal—some probably secretly hoped for a beam to fall on him. When he exited, however, coughing hard and blackened with soot, he had in his hand only Grandmother's prayer book, the *Korban Mincha.* Seeking her out, he handed it over. Then, before she could properly thank him, he vanished up the street. From that moment on, although Puttermilch did not change his profession or become a saint he gained a kind of spiritual respectability in the eyes of our community. I was to hear the story of "Puttermilch and the Prayer Book" over and over as I grew up.

In 1938 the Poles, imitating the Germans, established their own concentration camp at Kartus-Bereza. Puttermilch was the first person from Zdunska Wola to be sent there. When he returned in the spring of 1939 he was a broken man, a shell, who refused to tell anyone what had happened to him in Kartus-Bereza and whom people in our community pitied and began to care for with small, occasional gifts. Grandmother sent him challah for the Sabbath every week, continuing the practice until he disappeared when the Germans invaded Poland. No one knew where he had gone or why, or even if he had left of his own free will. I never saw Puttermilch again after August 1939. To me, he will be forever linked neither to crime nor to the Black Hand, but to the town hall fire and the edition of the *Korban Mincha* that I saw on Grandmother's reading table all the years of my childhood.

Grandmother's decision to send Puttermilch challah for the Sabbath did not surprise me, for I had known her to do similar things for other indigent people or families. After I turned ten but before I was sent to the yeshiva in Kalisz in September 1934, she would often ask me to ferry challah or other food to this or that street address and apartment number. On late Thursday afternoons, or sometimes on early Friday afternoons, following Grandmother's instructions, I would knock on unfamiliar doors in unfamiliar buildings, wait until I heard a sound, and then withdraw. I did not allow myself to be seen, for Grandmother did not want to call attention to her charity. Most of the families, I am sure, never knew the identity of the donor of their weekly challah.

She had her own special relationship with our town's rebbes and with God. She was not disrespectful or blasphemous, but neither did she see any reason to be passive in their presence. When most people in Zdunska Wola visited their rebbes, they did so in order to discuss a personal crisis, ask for a blessing, or, more rarely, ask for the rebbe's intervention. Most were content to receive a blessing and perhaps some words of comfort. Not Grandmother. When she visited the rebbe, she went with a specific goal in mind. Gradually working the conversation around to the topic of the desired goal, she would angle for her predetermined pronounce-ment or decision, not stopping until she received it. Her skill was famous and much admired in Zdunska Wola and the surrounding communities. I can only imagine how worried a rebbe must have been to hear Masha Tyger in his anteroom, requesting an audience.

If her conversations with the rebbes of Zdunska Wola were directed dialogues, her talks with God were often impassioned arguments. Prayer for her, as for many Jews, was not a one-sided affair. God was always present, and I would not have been sur-prised if she sometimes forgot herself and unconsciously reached out to try to touch God's sleeve. One day, in the early years of her widowhood and not long before I was born, the approaching Sab-bath caught her without money for Sabbath candles. Because she could not imagine greeting the Sabbath in this way, she pawned a mother-of-pearl button from one of her dresses and bought the needed candles. After lighting them, she prayed in her usual way, covering her eyes with her hands and talking directly to God. On this particular day her desperate circumstances overwhelmed her. Tears began to flow, then sobs, and then more tears. Unbeknown to her, for her eyes remained closed, a tear dropped onto one of the Sabbath candles and extinguished it.

After she finished praying, she opened her eyes and saw the darkened candle. Of course, having accepted the Sabbath she could not relight it. Now her talk with God, which earlier had been imploring and penitent, turned angry.

"Master of the Universe," she said. "You took my husband from me before his time. I did not complain. You scattered my children, and those that are still here are hungrier than any child should be. I did not complain. You asked me to choose to spend my little money on either challah or Sabbath candles, and still I did not complain. And I chose the candles to praise your name and to greet the Sabbath in the proper way. But you just blinded the Sabbath in one of its eyes. How dare you do this to me?"

God was supposed to have answered her, but I don't remember how. Although my family repeated this dialogue to me several times when I was very small and marveled at how Grandma had argued with God, I eventually suspected the story to be apocryphal. I had come upon similar stories when I studied with Reb Mendel and in the yeshivas in Kalisz and Warsaw. In those accounts, although the basic structure is the same, the dialogue and the detail are somewhat different and the ending is much more pointed. Most conclude by relating that another tear falling from the old woman's face is so hot that it rekindles the Sabbath candle.

Wondering about these stories and Grandmother's contentiousness toward God, I asked Reb Mendel what he would think if her Sabbath candles and tears story were indeed apocryphal. What if, I asked, it were only one of the many *bubemayses* (grandmother stories) that were part of Jewish culture? Reb Mendel did not seem disturbed by that possibility or by the possible intertwining of her story with other legends. "It is the spiritual truth of this story that matters," he told me, "and I believe that your grandmother probably does have arguments just like that with God."

I then asked why women rather than men light the Sabbath candles. "After all," I told Reb Mendel, "when Moses finishes building the Temple, isn't he given one more command by God? To light the menorah?" He responded:

That is correct. But remember that when the Temple was destroyed, the light of the menorah was snuffed out. In truth, however, the light had only become invisible, for it was parcelled out to the women of Israel for them to keep throughout the diaspora. The light is invisible most of the time because it is sacred. It becomes visible only when the Queen Sabbath descends into the world, summoned by Jewish women who illuminate, through the Sabbath candles, a universe shrouded in darkness. So your grandmother had a central role to play, Isaac, in the drama of the Sabbath, and she must have felt, or all the old women behind her must have felt, that if she was playing her role, then God should play his and allow the Sabbath candles to light up the universe, as they are supposed to.

Reb Mendel also helped me understand Grandmother's views on familiar biblical stories. One day, some time after I had returned from the yeshiva in Kalisz, I went to her apartment on a Sabbath afternoon to share some Sabbath fruit. When I opened the door, I found her sitting in her chair, bent over the *Tsena U'rena* and crying. She made no effort to hide her tears. At first I was afraid that she had had some sort of attack.

"Grandma," I asked. "Are you sick? Why are you crying?"

"I have been reading the story of Joseph and his brothers again," she said, "and it makes me very sad."

I was astonished. Up to that point in my life, the story had never affected me that way. Identifying with Joseph, I saw it as a tale of triumph over adversity, of success due to talent and industriousness despite the envy and plots of others.

"Why am I crying?" she asked, more of herself than of me. "A seventeen-year-old boy not much older than you is sold by his own brothers into slavery. After the Ishmaelites take him to a kingdom far away, his own brothers dip the boy's tunic in blood and give it to their father, allowing him to believe that a wild beast has devoured his favorite son. And so Jacob tears his clothes, puts on a sackcloth, and mourns for many, many days. He refuses to be comforted and intends to die weeping."

"But Grandma," I answered, remembering conversations with classmates in the yeshiva, "at the end, Joseph becomes the viceroy of Egypt and saves thousands of people, including his own family. Isn't that a good ending? Isn't that happy?"

"A happy ending?" she said. "What is that? For more than twenty years Jacob hears nothing about his son. Jacob believes that Joseph is dead. How can you ask why I am crying?"

"But still, Grandma," I insisted. "At the end the family is re-united and all is well."

"They may be together again, Isaac, but do you really think that all is well? No family can survive that sort of betrayal among brothers or such thoughtless pain inflicted by children on parents. And do you think that Jacob could possibly have been happy in Egypt? For the last seventeen years of his life he is a stranger in a strange land, and at the end he begs Joseph to take his corpse back to the land of his fathers so that he can be buried among his people. Among our people, Isaac. And what about Egyptian bondage of the children of Israel? What about four hundred years of slavery?"

These words came in an impassioned rush. I didn't know how to answer. She looked at me for a minute through her tears, then wiped her face and went into the kitchen. She returned with the fruit, and we talked no more about Joseph and his brothers that day or any other.

The intensity of her sorrow began to gnaw at me. Turning it this way and that in my mind, I soon decided that I had to ask Reb Mendel about it. He listened quietly until I had told him the whole story. Then, in the soft voice of a patience both infinite and kind, he said:

Your grandmother has had a life more difficult than you can now imagine, Isaac, though you will understand some of these things when you get older. Her sorrow is sometimes greater than she can bear. In the Talmud it is said that the gates of prayer are never locked. And that is true. But sometimes the gates of prayer may be closed, and it is at these most difficult times that the gates of tears are still open. The gates of tears are always open when words are not enough. Because your grandmother knows how to pray with her heart, she can talk directly to God, and without words. She prays with *kavannah* (devoted concentration).

I thought about that a while and then said, "But Reb Mendel, she was not praying then. She was reading a story about something that happened thousands of years ago." He responded:

Ah. Her reading was a form of prayer. And surely, Isaac, you remember the two sayings that are linked together: "Whatever happened to Jacob also happened to the people of Israel. Whatever happened to Joseph also happened to the people of Israel." That story is about a father or any parent. And it is about a son or any child. What happened to both of them was tragic, and for very different reasons. Now you see Joseph's side. Later you will also see Jacob's side. And the happy ending is small compensation for what the entire family went through. I sometimes think that the happy endings of such stories are there because they give comfort to people who cannot face so much sorrow directly. Your grandmother is able to face sorrow, and she does so through her tears. She understands pain. There is wisdom in understanding pain. There is wisdom in praying to God without words.

I was fourteen. I understood Reb Mendel's sentences but not their meaning and would not for a long time. In a few weeks he returned to the theme of tears in another context. That conversation took place early one morning after I had finished explaining a page of Torah to him. I thought we were finished for the day and had begun to put away my books. When I noticed that he had not moved, I looked at him, waiting.

"Do you remember," he asked, "the story about the golden chalice of tears?"

"Of course," I answered, wondering why he wanted to talk about the *becher* (wine goblet) story now. We had finished that discussion several months before.

"Tell it to me," he said.

"In the inner chamber of the heavenly tribunal," I began,

"there is a golden chalice in which the tears of Jewish children, all of them innocent victims, are gathered. According to the legend, when the chalice is filled the Messiah will come to the world and redeem the Jewish people and all of humanity."

"Very good," Reb Mendel said. "Now, do you remember what you asked me and what I said?"

"I asked you if there hadn't been enough innocent Jewish children slaughtered by now. Weren't there enough tears to fill the chalice? How was it possible for it still not to be filled? And you answered that Satan was at work, too, and that secretly he had made a tiny hole in the chalice through which tears have leaked out. That was why, for all the space of time up to the present, the chalice had never been filled."

"I know that my answer did not satisfy you," Reb Mendel replied, "although you didn't say anything. Can you tell me your doubts now?"

I took a deep breath, for this was unusual behavior on Reb Mendel's part. "It's not that I was dissatisfied. But I did not understand how Satan could so easily get into the inner chamber of the heavenly tribunal in the first place and, without God knowing it, make a hole in the chalice. Or, if God did know it or find out about it, why did he allow it?"

"These are the doubts of a good and inquiring student," Reb Mendel said. "Our fathers tell the story of the chalice in this way for a very specific reason. They want us to see that evil can be found within the very heart of good. Goodness is almost never completely impermeable to evil. The tears of children represent sorrow at its most pure. Yet even that most pure sorrow is not enough to redeem the universe. Perhaps the tears of others, especially the tears of righteous people, are needed as well to counteract evil. The Talmud says that whenever someone sheds tears over the suffering of a decent person, those tears are counted by God and put in his treasure house."

Reb Mendel did not mention my grandmother. He sat motionless. In the deepening silence between us I began to understand tears.

I always went to see Grandmother upon returning to Zdunska Wola from study in Kalisz, Zgierz, and Warsaw. She seemed always to know, before I even opened my mouth, what had been happening to me and how I was feeling. Usually, she greeted me with a strong embrace, and I reciprocated.

In 1937, under the influence of the Rebbe's Court in Zgierz, I returned in a different frame of mind. I had become rigidly pietistic and for months had been holding myself aloof, shunning all contact with women. On that late summer day, when she greeted me with a hug and kiss I moved back. Surprised, she tried again. Again I moved back. She then gave me a very long look. I expected a tongue-lashing, but her eyes twinkled and she laughed. Recognizing my behavior as excessive piety and fear of normal adolescent urges, she said, "It's no use, Isaac, es läuft, es läuft, es wird shoin überläufen (the pot is boiling, boiling, and it will soon boil over)."

On September 10, 1939, after a week of fleeing through the countryside, my family and I returned to Zdunska Wola. We learned almost immediately that Reb Mendel, Abraham Ozorowicz, and Avrum Yiedel Hirschberg had been executed. As soon as I could, I ran to Grandmother's apartment. She knew why I had come the moment she opened the door. Taking me into her arms, she said, "Wein, mein kind, wein. Du host ferleuren ein teiren fraind un ein guten rebbe (Just cry, my child, cry. You have lost a dear friend and a good rebbe)." And I did cry, for hours.

The German occupation changed everything. Of course, Grandmother's standing, like that of every other Jew in town, diminished considerably among the ethnic Germans and Poles. Before the war, even the Poles feared and respected her. Family lore often repeated her response to one Polish official, a known

anti-Semite who had warned her to pay special attention to a new
decree about small businesses: "Since when did you become in-
spector general? I remember when you lost your first tooth." Now
things were different. Yet through all the annoyances, depriva-
tions, and humiliations of daily life under German occupation
she kept her dignity and calm. Some in our community even began to envy her, for as soon as the war broke out she started regularly receiving packages from a niece who lived in Sweden, Ester
Freudmann. They contained coffee, sugar, chocolate, marmalade,
a bit of money, and sometimes a book or a two. Addressed to
"Widow Masha Tyger," the modest packages brought her specifically to the attention of the Germans sooner than otherwise
might have been the case.

One day in early fall of 1940, she was summoned to appear at
German headquarters. There, she was told that she and a number of other senior citizens of Zdunska Wola had been chosen to
be the guests of the Reich for two weeks at a special spa not far
from there. She had been chosen, they said, because of her age
and standing in the community, and she was asked to pack a suitcase and be ready to depart three days hence. Returning home,
talking the matter over with my mother and father, and making
inquiries in our community, she learned that every person being
sent on this "vacation" had one thing in common besides age:
Each periodically received packages from relatives or friends in
foreign countries. We decided later that the Germans must have
wanted to keep the packages for themselves.

On the morning of the appointed day, our entire family gathered in Grandmother's apartment. So did an unmarried aunt and
another aunt with her family. Two of Grandmother's closest
friends were there, too, and a neighbor as well. None of Grandmother's sons and their families were present, for they no longer
lived in Zdunska Wola. My little sister Yachet, four, stood at the

window, awaiting the arrival of the *kareta* (horse-drawn open cart) that would take Grandmother to the train station. Because no one was then being allowed out of the ghetto just to accompany a family member to the station, she would go alone. My aunts and my mother and father put on a cheerful front and smiled as they spoke of how rested Grandmother would feel after a two-week vacation at the spa.

Grandmother paid little attention to these remarks. Looking back, I think that she was the only one of all of us who knew that she would never return. Out of the corner of my eye, I noticed Yachet gesture to our sister Luba, who was not much older than she. I went over to the window and stood there with them. A kareta came crawling down our street, followed by two impassive German solders, and stopped in front of our building. I recognized the Jewish ghetto policeman who held the reins, Srulik Gerszonowicz. He was a distant cousin. Two elderly people were already in the cart, their suitcases at their feet.

When Srulik got off the cart and walked toward our building door, I turned and said to everyone in the room, "The kareta is here." My grandmother then said goodbye to us one by one, holding each person close and whispering something to each. She embraced my mother, her eldest child, for a long time, and quiet tears began to roll down her cheeks. The tears did not seem to alter her face in any other way or even affect her voice. They were just there. She came to me last and said, "Isaac, please take my suitcase to the street."

Outside, she stopped and looked back at the window, at her three daughters and their families, at everyone. Her eyes lingered on each face. Then she turned and embraced me, and I embraced her. "Good-bye, my Itsekel," she whispered, "my studious one, my little rebbe, you have my blessing. Remember the many psalms and praise God always. Study Torah with diligence and

PART TWO
IN THE GHETTO

F O U R
Hanukkah in a Monastery

December 1940. We had heard nothing from my grandmother since she had been taken away. The ghetto now contained about eleven or twelve thousand people, two or three thousand of them Jews brought in from outlying towns. Reb Sender, his wife, and their two teenage daughters shared our two-bedroom apartment with my mother and father, my four sisters, my brother, and me. They slept in the kitchen, on the floor and on a cot they had brought with them and rolled out at night when they created a private space by putting up a sheet between the two families. We had become accustomed to strangers using our kitchen as their bedroom, to food shortages, to the yellow star on our clothes, to the harsh voices, cold eyes, and fists of the German occupation forces, to rumors about Germans leaving Zdunska Wola, and to rumors about Germans not leaving Zdunska Wola.

What made everything even harder now, however, was the cold. In this, our second winter under the paw of the German beast and the first since the ghetto had been established, we had less to eat. The cold penetrated to our bones. Coal was also harder to get. Guitel and Esther, my two elder sisters, sometimes stood for hours in one of the several coal lines of the town and considered themselves lucky if they got a lump or two. More often, all they got was pinches from the Poles who lined up behind them and, knowing that they dared not leave the line, rubbed up against them. Mother and Father did not know of the abuse until one morning, when, as the girls were putting on their coats to go to the coal line, Esther began to tremble and then cry.

After that, getting coal became my responsibility and that of my younger brother Yossel. Sometimes we went together, sometimes we went to different lines. Although we tried various tactics, we were never as successful as Guitel and Esther, but they at least were no longer being groped. They now began trading with some of the Poles and ethnic Germans who had been customers of my grandmother and my father before the German invasion. A measure of calm returned to my sisters' faces.

And so Yossel and I began our dealings with the coal mongers of Zdunska Wola. Early one December morning, after I had waited for hours in line, I was told that there was no more coal. That was clearly a lie, because some was still visible in the bin. Behind me, however, stood several large Poles, and I knew it would be pointless to argue.

On my way home that cold December morning, depressed by my failure and not paying much attention to where I was going, I wandered into a relatively unfamiliar neighborhood. When I realized where I was, the yellow star on my jacket began to feel very large. As cold as I was from the biting wind, my awareness of being in a hostile part of town made me even colder. Then I saw something I had not noticed before: a small monastery, its courtyard gate slightly ajar. I had never been inside either a church or a monastery; as a yeshiva student, I did not enter churches and didn't know much about Christian rituals. Yet the half-open gate beckoned. "Just for a minute," I said to myself, "until I thaw out. And then I can continue home."

I slipped through the gate, crossed the courtyard, and entered a dimly lit chapel. It was empty. Although small, it seemed large to me then, for it was larger than our own stiebel or even that of the Gerer Hasidim, the largest Hasidic group in Poland, whose rebbe lived in Ger. On the altar stood a triptych of scenes that, I concluded, depicted the life of Jesus. The woman with an infant at her breast must be Mary, I thought. I also noticed a picture of the Crucifixion. After wondering how Reb Mendel would describe these representations, I sat down in a forward pew and took off my jacket so the yellow star was hidden. Long before, I had cut off my earlocks, hoping thereby to look more like a Pole or at least to draw less attention to myself. I must have sat there, alone and in silence, for twenty minutes. I began to wonder whether anyone was in the building and whether all chapels were this abandoned. In our stiebel, someone would be studying at every hour of the day. Gradually my limbs thawed.

I was about to stand up when I felt a hand descend on my left shoulder. I had heard nothing, no footsteps, no breathing, nothing. He was just there. He kept his hand on my shoulder as I turned to look at him. I knew that I shouldn't move, get up, or try to flee. "And now the Gestapo," I said to myself, "for being in a forbidden place." But the monk's face was kind. "My son," he asked softly, "are you hungry?" I nodded. He gestured for me to follow him. I walked behind his billowing, thick, dark robe, out of the chapel and down a long, bare corridor.

The silence seemed to intensify as we went further into the monastery. We crossed a small courtyard and came to a low pig shed. He led me inside and asked me to sit and wait for him. I sat and looked at the pigs in the shed with me. They appeared content and well fed. They were obviously indifferent to the German soldiers occupying Zdunska Wola. For a moment, just for a moment, I wanted to be one of those pigs. I wanted not to wear the yellow star, not to stand in endless queues, not to see my mother and father growing more lined and haggard every day, and not to kowtow to every German I saw. If I had prayed at that moment, I would have prayed for God to turn me into a pig.

The monk returned with a bowl of potato soup. "I am Brother John," he said, handing me the bowl and a spoon. "Eat in peace." He watched as I squatted on the floor and ate until my spoon scraped bottom. Then, from somewhere in the vastness of his robe he took out a piece of bread and gave it to me. I wiped the bowl with that bread until the entire surface shone. Watching my eyes and moving slowly, Brother John reached for my jacket, which still was inside-out on the floor beside me. His finger traced the outline of the yellow star. It was barely visible to the eye, although its six points were unmistakable to the touch. "Master of the Universe," I silently prayed, as soon I saw Brother John's index finger on the star, "I didn't mean what I wished for earlier about wanting to become a pig. Please don't punish me for that."

"I see that you are a Jew," Brother John said.

I nodded, not trusting my voice. At any moment I expected either to be tied up and handed over to the Gestapo or booted down the corridor through the chapel and out the courtyard gate. At least, I thought to myself, I had eaten a meal.

Then, only half intending to say what I said, I blurted out, "Perhaps these pigs need looking after. I could also help around the monastery. I could sweep and clean and light the stoves in the mornings. I am used to getting up early."

"Oh?" said Brother John, "and why does a young boy like you get up so early?"

I told him about my duties at the stiebel, about lighting the stove every morning at five, and about Reb Mendel and my many months of study with him. After recounting how Reb Mendel had died, I fell silent again, thinking that I had said too much. The silence between us grew.

Finally Brother John said, "We could use a boy like you, but you must promise me two things. First, while you work for us you must not leave the monastery. Second, you must tell no one else here that you are a Jew. And, of course, you must not mind sleeping out here with the pigs."

I told him that I would agree to those conditions after I had spoken with my mother and father, for I did not want them to worry about my sudden disappearance. Brother John asked me not to tell my parents where I would be or even that I would be working in a monastery, any monastery. I agreed to that, too, and with some relief, for I was sure that my father would have been upset to know that I was working in a Christian house of worship.

That very afternoon, after assuring my parents I would be safe, I came back to the monastery. Before entering through the same half-open gate, I carefully looked around to make sure no one had seen me. In a small satchel I had packed a toothbrush and one change of clothing as well as my phylacteries and a prayer book. As dangerous as it was to bring the very things that would betray my origins, I did not consider leaving them behind. Brother John was waiting for me in the chapel. Together we walked down the same long corridor as that morning. The silence now felt inviting and safe.

In the pig shed, I noticed that Brother John had brought in some new straw and heaped it in a corner, along with two thick blankets. After bringing me another bowl of potato soup, this time with some kind of meat in it, and a piece of bread and cheese, he said good night and left me alone. Despite the cold, the blankets were sufficient protection, because I slept buried in the straw rather than on top of it. In the morning I hid my satchel under the straw and began my duties. I scrubbed floors, cleaned the kitchen, and lit the stoves every morning at five. I fed the pigs and cleaned the shed once a day. Every morning also, as soon as it was light enough for me to see my hand and I knew that I was alone, I would say my morning prayers.

None of the other ten or twelve monks spoke to me. I don't know what Brother John told them, but it must have satisfied them, for none paid attention to me—none, that is, except Brother Peter. His dark and sad eyes, set close in a thin face, narrowed when he saw me, and soon I began to fear that he would report me to the Gestapo. But aside from staring at me at odd moments during the day, Brother Peter said and did nothing, and within three days I felt relatively secure in the monastery. Although I missed my family, I was glad to live without daily fear and grateful to have enough to eat. Every day the soup had meat in it, and some of it tasted unfamiliar, I decided not to worry about that. The first week passed quietly. I felt increasingly at ease until I remembered that in two evenings it would be Hanukkah.

The burden of that thought coincided with a request that the monks made, and the confluence of the two disturbed me. One morning, Brother John asked me to take the place of a regular altar boy who was ill. Of course, I could not refuse, and I trembled as I put on the clothes of the absent altar boy, wondering what I would be asked to do. Immediately I regretted not having paid more attention to the boys. Although they were my size, they were somewhat younger, and I had not spoken to them since entering the monastery. I had not even watched them as they went about their duties. They regarded me, I hoped, as some sort of peasant boy brought in to do the heavy work of the monastery. At any rate, they paid me as little attention as I paid them.

Now I also began to regret having entered the monastery in the first place. Here I was, a yeshiva student, about to participate in church worship. I felt doubly hypocritical, first because I was pretending to be a Christian in the company of people who were believers and second because I was a Jew. I wondered what the law said about my actions. I racked my brain but had difficulty finding something that discussed my situation. So I did as I was asked. Yet when I carried a portrait of the Madonna, I hoped Reb Mendel was not watching. I also sought to ease my conscience by talking to the figure in the painting, "You're a Jewish mother. You understand, don't you?"

My silent comments to an image on canvas somehow eased my mind, but I soon experienced other moments of unanticipated theological delicacy. As I stood at the altar with the other boys and heard the mass being conducted, I tried to counteract that influence by whispering Hebrew prayers under my breath. By far my greatest fear was that I would be asked to carry the crucifix. That action, I was convinced, could not be balanced by Hebrew prayers on my part. Fortunately, I did not have to face the prospect of such apostasy, for after three days the ill boy returned to the monastery and I returned to scrubbing floors, lighting stoves, and feeding pigs.

At the same time I was carrying the Madonna, I was wondering how I could celebrate Hanukkah in the monastery. Hanukkah had wonderful memories for me. I remembered my father's father polishing the menorah. I remembered how wonderful the contrast felt between the cold outside and the warmth inside. Although Hanukkah was not a major holiday in my community, it was celebrated with joy. We all loved the melodies, the succession of quietly festive nights, the light of the candles illuminating the darkness, the story of the oil that miraculously burned for eight days, and the fact that it was both a festival of light and a festival of peace.

Again, I began to miss my family and resolved to take advantage of my special circumstances. Carefully, I began gathering wax from the drippings of the votive candles. After I had enough, I made one candle, using for a wick one of the fringes from my *tallis-kattan* (prayer shawl), which I had worn under my shirt since entering the monastery. Jewish custom requires that the *tzitzis* (fringes) have eight ends, but seven are also acceptable, so I felt it was kosher to use one as a candlewick. I also was concerned about taking wax meant for the Virgin Mary and St. Teresa and transforming it into a Hanukkah candle. Here I found justification in a talmudic law that states that when something is thrown away it is no longer owned by anyone, so the drippings from the votive candles were no longer the property of the monastery, the Virgin, or another saint. The wax, that is, no longer belonged to anyone, and thus making a Hanukkah candle from it was permissible.

Once I had made the candle, I wondered where I could celebrate the ritual of Hanukkah. A light, even from a candle, would surely be noticed, and my singing might be heard. I began to look around the monastery. Every place I considered seemed too public. Then I discovered that one of the smaller buildings used as a dormitory for the monks had a trap door leading to a small attic. The trap door was used by chimney sweeps. Entering the attic, I felt my way in the darkness along the woodwork until I reached an open space next to the chimney, a crawl space large enough for me to stand. My head brushed the roof beams. My fingers felt along the chimney and found a narrow ledge about half a brick in width, right where the chimney narrowed. Lighting a match, I surveyed my domain. For the first time since beginning to live at the monastery I felt at home. No one would bother me here. Taking my crude candle from my pocket, I lit a match to its bottom. As soon as the wax melted, I placed the candle on the ledge, pressing it into the brick. The light from my Hanukkah candle cast a gentle shadow.

Almost delirious with joy, I began to chant the Maoz Tzur. For just a moment I was back home and younger in age. I could feel my grandfather's gentle pinch on my cheek, I could see my grandmother smiling, and I could hear my father's voice begin to soar. The monastery vanished. My struggles with the Madonna and the crucifix faded.

So concentrated was I on the traditional Hanukkah song that

I heard neither the creak of the trap door nor the shuffling of feet. But suddenly I saw my shadow cast on the chimney in front of me and turned to see the intense, narrow stare of Brother Peter. I knew he had heard me singing the Maoz Tzur. I wasn't frightened as I turned to face him, although I don't know why I wasn't. Perhaps I had become accustomed to the intensity of Brother Peter's dark eyes, or perhaps I sensed a bond between us. We stood and looked at each other for a long, long minute.

Just as I was about to blurt out some improbable explanation, Brother Peter said, "Let us sing together, let us sing the Maoz Tzur." And so we did. Brother Peter knew the Hebrew words and the melody. We sang about wanting to reestablish the Temple and to rededicate the altar. We sang about the troubles in Egypt and Babylonia. We sang about the plans for the oppression of the Jews by Haman and by the Greeks and about the seven shepherds who would conquer Israel's enemies. As we sang, I watched our shadows on the wall. For a moment, just a moment, they seemed to merge into one.

I did not ask Brother Peter why he knew the melody, and he did not volunteer a reason. The next morning, I did not tell Brother John about Brother Peter and the singing, but I knew I had to leave the monastery. I told Brother John that my family needed me at home and that I felt I had to return. He thanked me for my work and told me that I could return whenever I liked. I thanked him and said that my father would call him one of the righteous men. Brother John blushed but said nothing.

I left the monastery that morning through the same half-open courtyard gate through which I had entered. As I left, I was very much aware that I had received one of the rarest gifts of life in the ghetto: kindness from a gentile stranger. In December 1940 any acts of kindness toward Jews would be punished in some way; by 1941 the punishment would be much more severe and specific. By then, anyone in Poland caught aiding a Jew outside the ghetto, either by offering food or lodging or transportation, would be subject to the death penalty. But I would not know of that decree, proclaimed in November 1941, because by then Yossel and I were in our second labor camp, the St. Martin's Cemetery Camp in Poznan.

I was home for the final night of Hanukkah. As we sang the melodies, I thought of Brother John and Brother Peter and of my weeks of peace under the shadow of war and occupation. The festival now seemed deeper somehow, denser, and richer. I did not imagine that it would be the last Hanukkah I would celebrate with my family.

F I V E

The Pact

My days in the monastery in December of 1940 were my only reprieve that winter. In the ghetto we were monitored more closely by the Germans than we had been before. It became ever more difficult for Guitel and Esther to trade for extra food or to buy it from gentile merchants and smuggle it back home. My brother Yossel and I were often rounded up by German troops and by the SS looking for men to do manual labor on this or that job. After being forced to work like this several times, I decided to "volunteer." One day, sent to do janitorial work at party headquarters in the center of town, I asked the janitor, an ethnic German named Ferdinand, if I could work there on a more permanent basis as his assistant. He said that I could work for him but that he could not pay me anything. That did not matter to me because I was never paid anything anyway, and so I began to work as Ferdinand's assistant.

My major task was to bring in the coal each morning from the coal shed in the back and build fires in the dozen or so heating stoves in that four-story building. Every morning, after I had warmed the building, the first thing the Germans did on coming in was to throw open windows and exclaim, "Frische Luft, frische Luft (fresh air, fresh air)," letting out much of the heat I had so carefully built up. Although their behavior annoyed me, inwardly I smiled as I remembered how different Reb Mendel's attitude was toward building a fire and toward the warmth from stoves.

I kept that job as long as I could because it also gave me the opportunity on occasion to grab something for my family. Every two weeks, if I felt that no one would be looking, I would meet Esther at the outside fence just after I had arrived in the early morning. Over the fence, I would hand her a large chunk of coal, which she would hide in her cloak and quickly walk home. Fortunately, we were never caught. Once in a great while I would sneak into the cupboard next to the kitchen and put a handful of sugar, coffee, or tea in my pocket. I did not do this too often, for it was dangerous.

At that party headquarters I saw German anti-Semitic writings for the first time. The commandant ordered me and several others to prepare the headquarters for an educational rally to be held that evening. So I decorated the hall with streamers and swastikas and placed a pamphlet on every chair. When no one was looking, I put one of the pamphlets under my shirt and took it home. That evening, we all read about *Rassenkunde,* about the superiority of the Aryan race and the inferiority of other races, especially the Jewish one. We were astonished and, if not for the fact that the authors of the pamphlets and their followers had control over our very lives, would have laughed at the half-baked ideas in those pages and pitied the poor people who believed such inanities.

One morning I saw a new sign on the glass of the front door of party headquarters: "Juden ist der Zutritt verboten (Access Is Forbidden to Jews)." From that moment on, I would violate the decree by crossing the threshold each morning. Afraid as I was, however, I kept going to my job until Ferdinand pulled me to one side. "Isaac," he said, "I am being criticized by party members for being too friendly to Jews. You can't work here anymore."

Ferdinand was right. I thanked him and left immediately. Although relieved not to have to cross that threshold again and grateful that I would no longer be tempted to risk my sister's life over a chunk of coal, I was also sorry to lose the job. It was indoor work, no one beat me, and Ferdinand had been as kind as he dared.

Our apartment building was at the back of the ghetto, and the building's back fence opened onto an empty field. Yossel and I would go through a loose board in the fence and across the field when we wanted to avoid the authorities. That was our route when we began attending meetings of the Hashomer Hatsair, a Zionist youth group we had recently joined. Being two years younger than I, not very fond of reading in the first place, and of a much more pragmatic turn of mind, Yossel soon became bored and dropped out of the group. His boredom with my friends highlighted the differences between us. Whereas I sometimes would be called "Yeshiva Boy," he was known as The Engineer because of his ability to solve practical problems and fix things.

I had been invited to join the group by Hanania Grossman, its acknowledged leader and a Zionist whose knowledge of psychology I much admired. He said that he wanted me to join the Hashomer Hatsair because, although the group was atheistic, he hoped to study Talmud with me. In exchange he offered to tutor me in secular subjects. I was flattered by Hanania's invitation and looked forward to studying Talmud with him and learning from him. My real reason for joining, however, was an interest in two of the group's beautiful and intelligent girls, Poryia and Bronka. Poryia Szmulevicz soon became my first girlfriend. It was a totally innocent love. I never found the courage to declare myself. I believed that she reciprocated my feelings, for she would tease me whenever I blushed in her presence. We were seldom alone together. Mostly, we all met as a group, irregularly and secretly in different houses or out in the fields so that, surrounded by shrubbery, we could be invisible to the Germans and the ghetto police.

One evening after a meeting, I was crossing the field on my way home some time after curfew when Srulik Gerszonowicz, our cousin in the ghetto police, stepped out from the shadows just before I had reached the board in our fence. "Aha," he said in triumph. "Caught you, my little Isaac."

He took me down to the ghetto police station, where they kept me overnight. The next morning I was interrogated in the presence of the chief of the ghetto police, a man named Pick who could speak German without an accent and who will be forever associated in my mind with the betrayal of collaborating with occupation forces. My questioner pulled down my pants and whipped me on my bare backside until it bled. I was warned not to be caught again violating curfew and also ordered to stop attending meetings of the Hashomer Hatsair.

"That is an underground movement," the interrogator accused.

"It is not," I answered. "We talk about different topics, and we get to meet girls."

"What do you discuss?" he demanded.

"We talk about the Torah and also about psychology," I replied.

He kept asking over and over what we had discussed, but I told him only about some of the religious texts. Although it was true that we were a Zionist group and sometimes debated what might happen if we attacked a German patrol with homemade weapons, we weren't a danger to anyone. In fact, only someone with an overactive imagination could classify us as belonging to an organized "resistance" or "underground" movement. Most of our conversations concerned books and ideas. And yet the week before we had discussed *Paris Aflame.* Knowing that my treatment would be ten times worse if I confessed that detail, I kept quiet. On being sent home that morning, I could barely walk and could not sit for a couple of days. It was the first of several "official beatings" I was to experience between then and the end of the war. The fact that it was a Jew who had whipped me made it hurt all the more.

Over the next few weeks, now more careful, we in the Hashomer Hatsair resumed our ghetto routines and meetings. Although life in the ghetto meant that we were always hungry, always afraid, and always looking over our shoulders, the fact is that our common ghetto experience deepened so much else. We dismissed the constant injustices and insults as inconsequential. We felt we had an inner light that the Germans could not extinguish. In our daily prayers we reminded ourselves that we were the chosen children of Abraham, Isaac, and Jacob. German rules, laws, and actions, we felt, were only temporary, whereas the teachings of Torah were forever. My friends and I were passionate about books and ideas, for these were the things of the spirit and the things that mattered. It was in the ghetto that I had my first deep intellectual friendship with someone who was not a yeshiva student, Hanania Grossman, and in the ghetto that I felt love for the first time for a girl who also cared for me.

In early May 1941, the Germans let it be known that a labor transport would soon be formed for a six-month job in another province. The ghetto was ordered to be ready at a moment's notice. The Germans preferred, they said, that we volunteer, but if there were not enough volunteers they would take us anyway until the full complement of six hundred strong young men was reached. All able-bodied men between the ages of sixteen and forty were potentially on the list. Neither Yossel nor I volunteered, but our parents thought we would be chosen because we were young and I had been identified as a troublemaker.

It was a bright, sunny morning, typical of late May in Zdunska Wola. Earlier that morning we had observed, as we had for weeks, yet another long train filled with equipment rumbling toward the East. Father was wrapped in his tallis and wearing his tefillin, reciting his morning prayers. Mother was dressing my younger sisters. Guitel and Esther were about to leave the apartment and begin their daily task of scavenging for food. Yossel was sitting on the floor, fixing a chair. Reb Sender and his family had also finished their meager breakfast and were sitting quietly in their part of the apartment, talking among themselves.

I had just finished breakfast, and Esther was teasing me about being lazy, for I was the last one to eat that morning. "I have a good excuse," I told her. "I was out late, studying Talmud with Hanania Grossman and learning about Alfred Adler." Although I had violated curfew once more in order to study with Hanania, I had not been seen or caught on my way home and was now feeling pretty good.

Just before eight, we heard a banging on the door. When we opened it, there stood three Jewish ghetto police. One of them was Srulik Gerszonowicz. "Get your knapsacks," Srulik commanded Yossel and me, "put everything in them that you need, for you are going on a work detail to another city."

It had become common in Zdunska Wola to be visited by the Jewish police in this way, and my brother and I saw nothing unusually ominous in the summons. We were both resigned to our fate yet hopeful for the future. Yet I cannot forget the eyes of my parents as we said good-bye and were led away. Surely they were sensing that this parting would be permanent. I, however, did not. Unlike Grandmother, who seemed to be memorizing everyone's face before she stepped into Srulik's kareta, I did not make a conscious effort to remember the faces of my mother and father, of my elder sisters Guitel and Esther, and of my four younger sisters, Hannah Malka, Mindel, Luba, and Yachet. I cannot recall whether or not Reb Sender and his family said anything.

Just before I went out the door, Esther, who two months earlier had told me that she had become an atheist, came up to me. "You have forgotten your tefillin," she said, placing them in my hand. "Here, put them in your knapsack."

Yossel and I were taken first to the ghetto police station, where we were given physicals. The doctor who examined us, Dr. Yakov Lemberg, was later to become one of the heroes of the ghetto. "You are both very fit," he told us, "and able to work."

We both interpreted that as good news. Then we were taken to a textile factory on the other side of town. Once owned by a Hasid of my stiebel, the factory had now been appropriated by the Germans and all the machinery had been cleared out. In this shell of a building, on the bare floor, we sat for three days and three nights together with six hundred other young men, the first transport from Zdunska Wola.

There, sitting on the floor, wondering what was going to happen to us, Yossel and I made our pact. We would try to stay together. We would help each other through every difficult moment. We would each be the other's keeper.

SIX

Purim Revenge

After deportation I soon lost touch with what was happening in the ghetto of my hometown. Subsequent transports to the labor camps around Poznan, where Yossel and I lived until August 1943, brought news infrequently. It was only after the war that I found out what had happened to some of my friends and family and to some of our town's most prominent citizens. I have mused often on the lives and fates of three of those citizens: Nochem Ellia Zilberberg, whose links to Zdunska Wola's underworld I viewed as exotic and dangerous; Shlomo Zelichowski, whose piety and gentleness always reminded me of my own Reb Mendel; and Dr. Yakov Lemberg, our family physician and as *Judenälteste* (leader of the Jewish Council in the ghetto) since 1939 one of the few men in that position to be trusted both then and in memory.

None of my friends in Zdunska Wola knew when Nochem Ellia Zilberberg, whose father was revered by my grandfather's generation as a talmudic scholar, acquired notoriety as a savvy criminal. By the time I met him in 1938 his reputation for toughness and the ability to deal with our town's other questionable characters had long been established. To me he looked utterly unlike other Zdunska Wola Jews. He wore western clothes, fashionably fitted to his thick body, which was muscular even in his fifties. He was clean-shaven. He had hard gray eyes. He ate nonkosher food publicly and had an enormous appetite. The story went that often he would order an entire goose and a keg of beer, and when they were brought to him he would put the keg between his legs and drink from it as he ate the goose, all of it.

Yet despite being so different from the rest of us, Nochem Ellia still behaved in some ways as a Jew. He even sent his two sons to study with the Gerer Hasidim. They became Torah scholars, like their grandfather. A man of contradictions, Nochem Ellia became, with time, also a man of transformations.

As a boy, Nochem Ellia used to tell anyone who would listen that he was not going to be as poor as his father. He intended to own a big factory in town. Asked how he was going to do that, he would reply, "Just wait and see." Nochem Ellia had chutzpah. Even back then, all Zdunska Wola knew it. Some time in adolescence, he turned to the dark side. He was clever enough never to get caught actually committing a crime, but occasionally, especially when there was a theft requiring skill and daring, he would be among the first to be brought to the police station. When our parents warned us to steer clear of the town's unsavory characters they would often mention Nochem Ellia by name.

One day in 1932 he disappeared. Rumors flew: He had been murdered by one of his associates and buried deep in the sand dunes five kilometers from town; he had joined the Russian army; he had gone to America. For years no one knew anything. Then in 1937 an aunt received a letter mailed from Hamburg, Germany. He was fine, he wrote, and had a good job as the business manager of a very profitable enterprise. He didn't tell her what it was, and that silence fueled speculation back in Zdunska Wola.

He was earning enough money, he added, to support himself in style and put some aside for a rainy day. Soon he would be sending money to her. As I learned later, he actually did.

Only after he returned to our hometown in 1938 did we discover the source of his income. He had been the business manager of a hotel in Hamburg that also rented out rooms by the hour to local prostitutes. We concluded that he had likely been forced to come home. In early October 1938 the Polish government had revoked the passports of the more than fifteen thousand Polish Jews then living in Germany, the order to take effect at the end of the month. Germany told Poland that it would not allow stateless Jews to live in its midst and rounded up fifteen thousand on October 27 for deportation back to their country. The crossing was to take place on October 29 at the border towns of Chojnice and Zbonszyn.

The two thousand sent to Chojnice were allowed to proceed to Kracow. But in Zbonszyn, where most had been sent, the Poles first refused to receive their own citizens. The Jews were obliged to stay in a no-man's land between the borders of both countries and could neither go on into Poland nor back into Germany. The stalemate continued for a while. People suffered from cold and hunger, for they were forced to remain out in the open and a light freezing rain had turned the ground to mud. Because each person had been allowed to keep only ten German marks upon leaving Germany, they could not buy anything or bribe anyone for better conditions.

Somehow Nochem Ellia went through Zbonszyn and arrived back in Zdunska Wola with considerably more money than that. He was more confident than ever. He had gained weight and solidity in Germany. Within a few days he landed a job as business manager with a Swiss firm called Schneidholz and Son. Fluent now in German as well as in Polish and Yiddish, he increased the assets of the company and got along well with his boss. Although he worked hard and was universally acknowledged to be very good at his job, somehow it wasn't enough for him.

That restlessness, I suppose, led him to his next transformation. One day early in 1939, he happened to be talking with a Mr. Fuchs, a local manufacturer whose weavers had threatened to strike. Mr. Fuchs was desperate, for he could ill afford a strike at this time. Nochem Ellia suggested himself as a possible mediator, for, as he reminded Mr. Fuchs, he had done some work as a mediator and strike-breaker before going to Germany in 1932. Mr. Fuchs accepted, and that evening Nochem Ellia and his associates broke a few bones and windows. The strike never materialized.

A few weeks later, the spinners—who collected different yarn from different spindles, a job requiring dexterity and skill—also began to talk about striking. Most were young and devout Hasidic men who had growing families to support but could barely do so on their earnings. One morning, just as they were gathering at the stiebel for prayers, after which they planned to talk about striking, Nochem Ellia came through the door.

"Good evening, my dear friends. I sympathize with your demands," he told them. "I remember the poverty of my own father. But is a strike the best solution to your problems? Think of what it would do to your families. The manufacturers could easily bring in spinners from out of town, and where would you be then? You would be out in the cold. You should really consider negotiating in a businesslike fashion. If you are interested, I will be an honest broker for you."

There was silence among the men. They all knew, however, what had happened to the weavers and decided to accept Nochem Ellia's offer. On that day he entered the kingdom of legend. Union representatives no longer went to their rabbis or priests to voice their grievances. They went to Nochem Ellia, who would find a way to settle the differences between management and labor. Often he intimidated merely through the glare of his cold eyes. Sometimes he used sweet words. When he thought it would be more effective to do so, he used force. Managers appreciated him more than workers did. Although the union leadership disliked dealing with him, they saw no other way of being successful in mediation.

Nochem Ellia had chutzpah. He also had what we called *protekcja* (special connections), for his Swiss boss supported him in everything and even ran interference for him with local authorities. In 1939, before the war, local police again were rounding up disreputable characters, this time in order to send them to a Polish concentration camp called Kartus-Bereza. Nochem Ellia was charged with counterfeiting and was sentenced, but the sentence was not carried out. Perhaps his boss pulled some strings, perhaps he bribed someone. In any event, Nochem Ellia remained among us. Then, in early August 1939, just as he had in 1932, he again disappeared and was not in Zdunska Wola when the Germans invaded Poland. In early December he returned. He never told anyone where he had gone or why. He simply resumed his duties at Schneidholz and Son and became even more indispensable to his boss, who now began to travel widely in search of business. Nochem Ellia became in effect the head of the company. When the Germans established the town ghetto, he was the only Jew allowed to live outside it, in a bungalow on the company's grounds.

Now began another transformation, this one as surprising as it was welcome to us. People began to hear of favors he did for others, favors sometimes so small that at first we wondered where the profit was. He would quietly get milk for a child or medicine for a sick woman. Either he would deliver the food or medicine personally, or he would have it delivered, mostly through a man he often used as a porter, Leib Rogozinski, never asking for payment. People began to call him Reb Ellia, and those who had turned their backs on him now greeted him openly. Some even pleaded with him for this or that necessity. In the minds of my family and others in the ghetto, he became almost heroic. Openly he began to speak of his love for Israel and the Jewish people.

Even his face changed; it became softer, kinder, and more compassionate, and his eyes lost their glare. Some said he had become a *baal-tshuva* (penitent). "Imagine that!" they said, "Nochem Ellia, the former strikebreaker, now cares what happens to other Jews." Others even claimed to have seen Nochem Ellia wrapped in his father's tallis and phylacteries, swaying and praying. I myself never saw him in prayer like this, although I believed such a transformation to be possible, for our family once experienced the kindness from Nochem Ellia that others spoke about. About a year before Yossel and I were deported, he sent our family some expensive medicine, through Doctor Lemberg, to treat my youngest sister. And he brushed aside my father's attempt to pay him.

Aided by special connections, his Swiss boss, Nochem Ellia tried to help the Jewish community continuously and succeeded in doing so until late 1941. He would go to police headquarters and inquire about someone's disappearance or interrogation. He would also ask about confiscated property. Sometimes he would say that it really belonged to the Swiss firm and that his own company had not been properly paid. Speaking in the name of his boss, he would give authorities the choice of either returning the property to the Swiss firm or paying for it. He would also present papers of ownership that he himself had forged, for now, of course, he was using his criminal talents for the benefit of others.

Gradually, however, as the ghetto was sealed off from the rest of the population, Nochem Ellia's influence waned and local authorities no longer treated him with deference. Early in 1942 he was arrested, along with his partner in smuggling, Leib Rogozinski, a simple man who generally worked as a porter. I remember Leib standing in the town square waiting for customers, his heavy rope circled around his waist and one shoulder. A day or so after that first arrest, other Jews were arrested and accused of engaging in criminal activities. And then the Germans arrested some Jews for not wearing the star of David arm band or for not greeting the authorities with the proper deference.

All Zdunska Wola panicked. Nochem Ellia's sons wrote the authorities and offered to pay a "tax" for his release. It was refused. Mr. Schneidholz tried to intercede. He, too, was rebuffed. What could the Germans be thinking? No one knew then that in a few days the Germans would follow a practice later called, with bitter irony, Goebbels's Jewish calendar—the public execution of Jews, often numbering ten and thus said to constitute a minyan, on or very close to a major Jewish holiday.

In 1942 Purim occurred on March 2, 3, and 4. A few days before, Doctor Lemberg received a visit from the Gestapo. Choose ten Jews from among the criminals who had been arrested, he was ordered, and they would be hanged in revenge for the hanging of Haman. Everyone caught the intended echoes to the Book of Esther, in which Mordecai's refusal to bow down to Haman, the righthand man of King Ahasuerus, became the "official cause" of the punishment of the Jewish people. Haman used Mordecai's action as the foundation for the order to annihilate all Jews in the kingdom of Ahasuerus.

Doctor Lemberg refused to choose ten Jews, and I am not sure who finally chose the so-called criminals. It was probably Pick, the chief of the ghetto police and, like all the ghetto police, a Jew. Next the council was ordered to select ten members of the ghetto police to act as hangmen. The Jewish police at first declined to participate, for they felt they would be ostracized and their families and children would suffer. Told that a refusal would mean that they themselves would be hanged, they decided that only those who were unmarried would act as hangmen. And so they drew lots.

On the Fast of Esther, before Purim itself, the sounds of hammering could be heard all through Zdunska Wola. In the marketplace of the ghetto and under the watchful eyes of German troops, several ghetto police put up the gallows—a single long beam about four meters from the ground and stretched between two solid posts braced by other, shorter posts. Again the council met and resolved to do everything possible to bargain for the lives of the ten men. Doctor Lemberg went to the Germans and offered to increase the work output of the ghetto. The proposal was refused, and the commandant, angered at Doctor Lemberg's persistence, told him that if he and the rest of the council continued their trouble-making, then all of the Jews of Zdunska Wola would be put to death. It was either these ten men or the entire community.

Doctor Lemberg was ordered to visit the ten men in their prison cell and inform them of the impending execution. When he did so, he told them that the choice was between ten and the entire community. Nochem Ellia received the news with joy. He said that their deaths would now have meaning. Nochem Jachimowicz, a quiet, dignified, and scholarly man of about sixty standing next to him, nodded in agreement.

Nochem Ellia began to sing. The other nine men joined in. They sang, Doctor Lemberg later reported to the council, with great strength. From his office, Pick shouted at them to shut up, but they paid no attention.

As Doctor Lemberg left the cell, Nochem Jachimowicz called after him, telling him to let the council know that the ten men considered their deaths to be *al Kiddush Hashem* (santification of the name of God), our tradition of martyrdom. Reb Mendel more than once discussed with me the story of Rabbi Akiba's martyrdom in the second century of the Common Era. In reprisal for yet another Jewish uprising, the Romans had made certain Jewish customs capital crimes, among them circumcision, the observance of the Sabbath, and the study of Torah. Some rabbis went underground, but Rabbi Akiba continued to observe the Sabbath publicly. Captured, he was tortured and sentenced to death. Before his execution, some of his students visited him in his cell.

"How did you stand the torture?" they asked him.

"By reciting the Shema," Rabbi Akiba answered. Asked how he could recite the Shema in such painful circumstances, Rabbi Akiba said that all of his life he had wondered whether he could actually fulfill the commandment from Deuteronomy and even in the worst moments love the Lord with all of his heart and soul and strength. He learned during the torture that he could, and so he would go to his execution without fear and in peace. The Talmud says that as he was being executed, he recited the final *echod* (The One) of the Shema just as his soul left his body and became one with God.

At nine on Purim morning, 1942, the Germans entered the ghetto and herded everyone, including the children, to the marketplace. There, eyewitnesses later said, a bizarre scene unfolded. Germans soldiers disported themselves, and many of the Poles and ethnic Germans gathered to gawk as if at a circus. In the center of the square, facing the gallows, all of Zdunska Wola's Jews stood in silent shock.

At about eleven on that sunny morning the ten condemned men arrived, led by the ten Jewish police who were to be their hangmen. They marched in silence, as soldiers would. Nochem Ellia appeared to be in command of the condemned. "We march," witnesses remember him intoning, "so that our enemies cannot detect in us even a trace of weakness."

Each marched up the three steps of the stepladder to the gallows and stepped onto the stool that had been placed under each rope. Each stood silent and straight as the rope was placed around his neck.

From among the assembled Jews, the Germans dragged out Doctor Lemberg and pushed him up the stepladder. Was he, too, going to be hanged? But no. Flanked by German officers, he was forced to stand on that stepladder and deliver a speech justifying the hangings. Speaking in Yiddish, he said before each sentence, "The Germans have ordered me to tell you that. . . ." He then delivered the official justification: The Jews were being hanged for their crimes against Germany, they were being hanged in revenge for Haman, they constituted a minyan, and this was how Purim should be celebrated. Everyone appreciated the courage behind his words, for he had no way of knowing whether the ethnic Germans in the square would reveal what he was actually saying. Many knew Yiddish but did not betray Doctor Lemberg. Twice he fainted. Twice he was revived and forced back up the stepladder to continue his speech. Each time, he asked the assembled Jews to be strong and not cry.

As Doctor Lemberg was finishing, Leib Rogozinski called out in a voice that echoed throughout the square, "Jews, avenge our blood. Take revenge on these lowly murderers."

Although the German commandant could not understand Leib Rogozinski's Yiddish, he was startled by the power and passion of his voice and by its lack of fear. "Hang them," the commandant shouted out. "Hang them now."

Leib Rogozinski and Nochem Ellia were hanged first. Each of the ten recited the Shema before the rope was tightened and the stool kicked from under their feet. The hangings were completed shortly before noon.

All day the bodies of the ten men remained suspended from their ropes and guarded by German troops, and all day people from the rest of the town were either brought by or came on their own to stare. Teachers brought their classes. Only with the approach of nightfall were the ten cut down and, under orders from the Germans, buried in a mass grave. The council's request to bury them in accordance with Jewish custom was refused.

Shlomo's Last Prayer

In many ways no one could be more different from Nochem Ellia Zilberberg than Shlomo Zelichowski. He dressed as a Hasid,
with an elegant black morning coat that went halfway down his
calf and was slit in the back. He was always cheerful, and his eyes
radiated kindness. Soft-spoken and gentle, pious and studious, he
was for other boys what Reb Mendel was for me—a teacher and
role model. He lived in Pabianice, which lay between Zdunska
Wola and Lodz, but after marrying the daughter of Benjamin
Rudal he came to our town often. When the Germans occupied
Poland, Shlomo Zelichowski moved his family to Zdunska Wola,
where they all lived in the home of his father-in-law.

Like Nochem Ellia, Shlomo Zelichowski had worked as a mediator before the war, but his methods were very different and he
never became involved in labor disputes. Perhaps his skill in mediation gave him insight into how to handle his own workers,
because he never had labor problems when he was a textile manufacturer in Pabianice. Asked about his secret, he would only say
that he always treated workers with respect: "I listen to their prob-

lems, and I never pay them less than other manufacturers do. I also welcome them into my home and never make them wait."

Others in the community, more piously inclined, said that there were two other reasons for Shlomo Zelichowski's good fortune: the beauty and passion of his voice when he chanted the blessings or sang the prayers on the major holidays and his ability to sound the shofar. No one else's voice could soar quite like his, a voice he inherited from his father, the much-loved Reb Moishe Gdalyahu. No one else's melodic rendition of the prayers penetrated as deeply to their spiritual essence, and no one else could sound the shofar in the same way. Still others said that the person responsible for Shlomo Zelichowski's standing in the community was his wife, for she baked the most delicious challah and applestrudel.

When the Zelichowski family came to live in Zdunska Wola in 1939, I was an adolescent and only somewhat attracted to the cantorial splendor of Shlomo Zelichowski's voice. Much more was I attracted to his beautiful daughter Zelda. At fifteen, she had a gentle voice and golden hair, deep brown eyes, and creamy skin. I was smitten. But I never said anything to her, for my yeshiva training made me uncomfortable with girls, and I barely knew what to say around them. She never spoke to me either, and I doubt she was aware of my feelings.

For a number of years, it was only our community and the town of Pabianice that knew of Shlomo Zelichowski's cantorial voice and his talent with the shofar. But in the early 1930s, as his fame spread and as he became an even more avid follower of the rebbe in Ger, Shlomo Zelichowski ceased to celebrate the High Holy Days in the Hasidic stiebel in Pabianice and began to spend them in Ger. Beginning in 1933 or 1934, about a week before Rosh Hashanah he would travel alone to Ger and remain there until after Yom Kippur. He fasted every Monday and Thursday. Each day he cleansed himself in the ritual bath and dispensed charity, all in preparation for leading the many worshippers in prayer. He was so charitable that he even had to borrow money to make the return trip home.

For the first two or three years everything went well, and Shlomo Zelichowski returned home full of praise and full of peace. But one year—it must have been 1937—at the conclusion of the Yom Kippur service, when Shlomo Zelichowski in his role as the official *baal t'kia* (sounder of the ram's horn) put his lips to the shofar to sound the *t'kia gedola,* nothing happened. Silence. He sighed, grunted, and puffed again and again. Finally, a few notes trickled out, but they bore no resemblance to the most significant of all the shofar notes, the t'kia gedola, the single, unbroken blast that carries the sound of eternity and is held as long as the blower's breath holds. It is the note that promises the coming of the Messiah. Ashen-faced, shoulders stooped, and hands trembling, Shlomo Zelichowski handed over the shofar to one of his assistants so the service could be concluded.

The next morning, he stood in line with other Hasidim, waiting his turn for an audience with the rebbe of Ger, Avrom Mordecai Alter. Like the others, Shlomo Zelichowski handed the rebbe a kvitl, a request for advice or intercession with the Lord. Shlomo Zelichowski did not ask for the usual things. He did not ask for better health, or for a dowry for his daughter, or for a better year financially. He asked only to be able to sound the t'kia gedola at next year's Ne'ila, the concluding service of Yom Kippur. The rebbe looked at the kvitl, and he looked at Shlomo Zelichowski and took his hand, but he said nothing.

"The rebbe's silence," Shlomo Zelichowski told my father when he visited Zdunska Wola later that fall, "means that the petition is not ripe enough, that I need to make myself worthy. I need to be kinder, more charitable, more compassionate."

"But how is that possible?" answered Father. "I cannot think of anyone more worthy than you."

The next year, 1938, Shlomo Zelichowski put his lips to the shofar and again failed. Once more he gave a petition to the rebbe of Ger. At first he said nothing, and Shlomo Zelichowski began to wonder where in all that silence he would find the answer. Then the rebbe spoke. What he said only puzzled Shlomo Zelichowski further. He repeated the conversation to my father.

"How is your daughter Zelda?" the rebbe asked.

"She is beautiful," answered Shlomo Zelichowski, "may no evil eye touch her."

"Is she learning the things a Jewish daughter must know?"

"Of course, she is following in her mother's footsteps with diligence and with great devotion."

"Are the young men beginning to come to the house on odd pretexts?"

"Yes."

"Such beauty can be a burden," the rebbe said, and then he fell silent. He said no more.

"Why," Shlomo Zelichowski asked my father, "is the rebbe asking these questions? After all, he has never seen Zelda, and I have never mentioned her as a problem. The truth is just the opposite. The rebbe knows that I have no son, but Zelda has been the blessing of my married life. She is so gracious, gentle, beautiful, and intelligent. Every day my wife and I thank the Holy One, blessed be he, for the gift of Zelda in our lives. Why should she be on the rebbe's mind now? What have I done?"

That night my father and mother tried to make sense of the rebbe's words. They turned the details over and over, polishing them like stones, and in this way I came to know much more about Shlomo Zelichowski's pain than I otherwise would have.

By 1940 neither Shlomo Zelichowski nor anyone else left our town during the High Holy Days. No one could celebrate in a synagogue, either, for they had all been burned or destroyed. By then we were gathering together in basements and attics and among friends. In fall of 1941, several months after my brother Yossel and I had been deported, Shlomo Zelichowski and his father-in-law, Benjamin Rudal, had some friends over to their house for the Kol Nidre service. In the middle of the whispered prayers, a loud banging sounded on the door. A member of the ghetto police and two soldiers stood there.

"Zelda Zelichowski," the Jewish policeman shouted out. "The Herr Major requires your presence."

Zelda stood up and left the room. Outside, the powerful purr of a German staff car lingered in the air as the car sped away. Everyone gathered around Shlomo Zelichowski and Benjamin Rudal, speaking words of comfort and wondering what could possibly be done. They did not resume the interrupted service.

It was late when Zelda came home that night. Through parted curtains, the neighbors watched her being escorted to the house by a German soldier and being embraced by her mother. She told her parents that the German major wanted her to work for him as a maid. She had answered that she had to ask her father for permission first. The major then gave her until the next morning for an answer. Shlomo Zelichowski and his wife prayed most of the night, but they knew what the answer had to be. The next morning, dressed in the plainest clothes her mother could find, Zelda began to do housework for the German major. For several weeks she left home early in the morning and returned home in the evening.

One day, however, Zelda did not come home for more than twenty-four hours. She told her parents that the Herr Major had given a large dinner party the night before and had ordered her to clean up after it. When she finished, it was too late to return home, so she had stayed in the maid's quarters in the Herr Major's house.

The next morning, Shlomo Zelichowski sent word to the Herr Major that Zelda was ill. For hours she and her parents discussed whether she should return to work. Finally, Zelda looked straight at her father and burst out, "The Herr Major says that if I don't do what he wants he will send you to a place from which you will never return! So you see, I have to go back. I have to."

As if awakening from a long sleep, Shlomo Zelichowski saw his daughter as she truly was that morning, saw the tears on her cheeks and the desperation in her eyes, and understood. He said no more that day, and neither he nor his wife spoke about the situation. Zelda went back to work the next morning, and from then on neither she nor her parents mentioned her work. It became part of the silent fabric of their altered lives.

People argued about whether Zelda's sacrifice was protecting her family or endangering it. Later they would argue about the possible connection between her activity and Shlomo Zelichowski's arrest late in the spring of 1942. Fear permeated the town with that arrest, for it was the first of ten arrests just before Shavuos. The ten men included Benjamin Rudal and several of the most prominent and pious men in our community. Even Mordecai Morgenstern, who before the war had owned the winery in town, was among the ten. These ten were thus somewhat different as a group than the ten of the Purim hanging. Although everyone wondered what official justification would be given for their arrests, no one believed that the Germans felt the need anymore for excuses. They would simply carry out the demented policies of their twentieth-century Haman. Everyone now feared the implementation of Goebbels's Jewish calendar. When the gallows went up, no one doubted what would occur.

As before, Doctor Lemberg was ordered to go the prison cell and tell the ten men that they were going to be hanged on Shavuos. "What shall I tell them is the justification?" he asked the commandant.

"Tell them that they are being hanged for smuggling and other crimes against the German nation."

"But these men are among the most pious of our community!" Doctor Lemberg protested. "They are honest men, every one of them, and none of them ever broke any law."

The commandant turned to a man in a clerical collar who was standing next to him in the office, someone he called the Reverend Wilhelm Weber. The pastor leaned toward him and spoke into his ear.

"Then tell them," the commandant said in clipped phrases, "that they are being hanged for the temerity of receiving the Ten Commandments, for the arrogance of believing that they are the chosen ones. Well, today I choose them in the name of the Führer. Reverend Wilhelm Weber informs me that Shavuos celebrates the Ten Commandments and therefore the birthday of the Jewish people. On that day this minyan of a deluded and arrogant people will die. You are dismissed."

That evening, Doctor Lemberg, visiting the ten men in their prison cell, told them the news and the rationale the commandant had given him. He said that he was sorry that he could not have done more for them, sorry that as the Judenälteste he had not finally been able to protect them and had not fulfilled his responsibility properly.

"Do not worry, my friend," answered Shlomo Zelichowski. "You have done all that could have been done. We have only one request of you and that is that you smuggle into this cell by tomorrow evening, because it will be the evening before Shavuos, everything that we need for a Shavuos service and for a Yom Kippur service."

"I will try," said Doctor Lemberg. "But Yom Kippur? We are so many weeks before Yom Kippur."

"We will do the concluding service of Yom Kippur, the Ne'ila. It may not be Yom Kippur on the calendar, but it is our day of judgment. We will stay awake all night on Erev Shavuos and pray. Tomorrow night we shall declare before the Holy One, blessed be he, that we ten are willing to atone for the sins of all the Jewish people."

Doctor Lemberg promised to do what he could. Early the next evening he returned with everything required, including a shofar. I don't know how he got past the Jewish police. Perhaps they were bribed. Perhaps they simply looked the other way. Or perhaps they collaborated with Doctor Lemberg, defying the danger to their own lives.

That evening, standing barefoot on a few reeds brought from the creek at the edge of the ghetto, reeds customarily used for decorating the altar on Shavuos, Shlomo Zelichowski led the nine other men in a full Shavuos service. He also chanted the Haftarah of the second day of Shavuos and recited the Yetziv Pisgam, which praises God as the giver of the Torah and the creator of the universe. After finishing the Shavuos service and prayers, he began the Ne'ila service of Yom Kippur. He opened it by retelling the story of Rabbi Joshua ben Levi, who found Elijah standing at the entrance to a cave.

"When will the Messiah come?" Rabbi Joshua asked Elijah.

"Ask him," said Elijah.

"And where is he?"

"He's at the city gate, sitting among sick people and beggars, and you will recognize him as the only one who removes his bandages one at a time."

"Why is this so?"

"He needs to be ready instantaneously, when called to begin the redemption."

And so Rabbi Joshua went to the city gate and found the Messiah, who told him that he would be coming that day. But he did not come that day. The next day, Rabbi Joshua asked the Messiah again, who again said that he would come that day but did not. On the third day, the pattern was repeated. The Messiah then explained. "Today, if the people of Israel repent wholeheartedly, then I will come."

"How do we repent wholeheartedy?" Rabbi Joshua then asked Elijah.

Elijah replied, "When you come to a house of worship you must not remain standing at the outer gate, but you must enter and go through gate after gate, until reaching the innermost gate. For the gates are made to be entered."

Shlomo Zelichowski continued, now with the main leitmotif of the Ne'ila, "Psach lanu shaar": "Open for us the gates, even as they are closing. The sun is low, the hour is late. Let us enter the gates at last. The sun is low, the hour is late. Let us enter the gates at last."

Word by word, prayer by prayer, the men made their way through the concluding afternoon service of Yom Kippur. Just before they got to one of the most beautiful of all the Ne'ila melodies, "God of awesome deeds, God of awesome deeds, grant us pardon, as the gates begin to close," Shlomo Zelichowski stopped. "Let us not sing this melody now," he told the others. "Let us reserve it for the march through the square to the scaffold."

The other men agreed. The hardened ghetto police, who throughout Shlomo Zelichowski's Yom Kippur service had remained in the yard of the jail, listening and even softly participating from time to time, began now to cry like children. Afterward, it was they who told others in Zdunska Wola the story of the last night of this extraordinary minyan. I have sometimes wondered if our relative in the ghetto police, Srulik Gerszonowicz, who had taken my grandmother away in the kareta and who had arrested Yossel and me, was among those policemen that evening.

The mystics say that at midnight on Shavuos the heavens open so that prayers and melodies can ascend directly to the heavenly throne. Precisely at midnight, the zero hour of the day on which he was to die, Shlomo Zelichowski sounded the shofar. The full, rich, and almost endless blast rang through the prison and echoed over Zdunska Wola. It reached some people who were still awake, for they had been praying and reciting the Psalms. It awakened others. Still others slept through the blast and insisted later that such a thing could not possibly have happened.

As the sound of the shofar, with its promise of the Messiah, lingered over the town, people turned to each other and asked, Why now? And who? And out of season? My father would have been awake praying that night, and I have often wondered what he must have thought on hearing the shofar. Would he have known that it was Shlomo Zelichowski sounding it, and would he have cast his mind back to the conversations between his friend and the rebbe of Ger? Would he have said that the rebbe's silence now delivered its answer?

All this, told to me by various people at various times and with different levels of detail, happened on that night in Shlomo Zelichowski's cell. And I transmit it here, but in truth I do not know what actually took place. We can never know. I do know that I shall always feel awe before such an extraordinary human being. Not even imagination can reach the spiritual heights experienced by those ten men in the night before they were to die.

As they had earlier on Purim, on the day of Shavuos the Germans herded all of Zdunska Wola's Jews to the square. Many Poles and ethnic Germans came also, and witnesses say that some German officers even brought their mistresses. Again, the Germans were festive. At the appointed hour the ten men were brought by the ghetto police. In addition to Shlomo Zelichowski, Mordecai Morgenstern, and Benjamin Rudal, the group was rounded out by David Chaskielewicz, Mendel Cohen, Hersh Lajzer Saburzsinski, Hershel Starzinski, Szaja Ber Sanator, Juri Pszecik, and Jehuda Szmul.

A hush fell over the crowd as the ten, their hands tied behind their backs, entered the square. Then a murmur arose, for the ten men were serene and at their head Shlomo Zelichowski was smiling, his face radiant. Many in Zdunska Wola had seen his face like that at the *bimah,* where a rabbi or cantor stands, ecstatic in prayer, but they did not expect it here.

The Germans intended with this hanging to teach Zdunska Wola a lesson in domination by the master race. But they failed because of Shlomo Zelichowski. As the ten men walked toward the gallows, he lifted his face to the sky and began to sing, in the voice that all Zdunska Wola knew and loved so well, the song from the Ne'ila service that the ten had agreed upon the night before. The nine men behind him, in strong and clear voices, joined in when he came to the refrain for the first time:

> El-nora alilah,
> el-nora alilah,
> hamtse lanu mechilah,
> b'shaath ha ne'ilah
> el-nora alilah.
>
> [God of awesome deeds,
> God of awesome deeds,
> grant us pardon,
> as the gates begin to close,
> God of awesome deeds.]

When he came to the refrain the second time, a number of the assembled Jews joined in. On the third repetition of the refrain, virtually all of the Jews—there were several thousand—were singing. The Germans were frantic. This had never happened.

Ten stools had been placed beneath ten ropes because the Germans planned to hang each man individually so as to draw out the grisly ceremony as long as possible. But the intended lesson failed to materialize. Approaching the first stool, Shlomo Zelichowski jumped on it immediately, smiled at the German soldiers and ghetto police, and said, "Nu (So)?" He motioned with his head to the rope above and stretched his neck toward it. "Nu?" he repeated.

Again, confusion. This, too, had never happened. Suddenly, in the emptiness of that stunned silence, Shlomo Zelichowski directed his voice heavenward and sang the Shema. Then he sang it again, and, as before, all the Jews sang it with him. Leibel Brikman, a survivor whom I have never met but whose eyewitness account has helped me to visualize this scene, says that everyone was exalted, everyone was lifted up, everyone cried without tears, and everyone called out the Shema from the innermost part of their souls.

After the hangings, the Jews in the square did not disperse. They stood in silent homage to their ten martyred citizens and in defiance of the Germans. Finally, with rifle butts and whips and dogs, the Germans, aided by the ghetto police, pushed the crowd out of the square. These ten men, unlike those hanged on Purim, did not remain on the gallows all day. The Germans permitted them to be cut down soon and be buried in accordance with Jewish custom.

Later that same year, underground newspapers in ghettos across Poland published accounts of the Shavuos hanging in Zdunska Wola. Although they praised all ten men, they turned to the actions of Shlomo Zelichowski again and again, asking how such a spiritual hero came to be. What did he imbibe with his mother's milk? How had he prepared himself and the nine other men for death? At the end of the war, in one of the Warsaw ghetto's secret underground archives, a poem written by Yitzhak Katzenelson was found: "The Song of Shlomo Zelichowski."

I have often tried to imagine my father, along with the rest of my family, in that town square on that fateful day of Shavuos in 1942. How would he have described it to me? What did he do? What did he feel, on seeing his friend martyred? My father of all people understood how Shlomo Zelichowski came to be a hero. But I have lost my father's eyes and ears, for after my deportation from Zdunska Wola in May 1941 I never saw him again.

The Judenälteste of Zdunska Wola

My brother Yossel and I speculated in Yunikowo, our first work camp, about what Dr. Yakov Lemberg must have been thinking that May morning in 1941 when, as the physician to the ghetto and as Judenälteste, he first selected us and then gave us and six hundred other men physical examinations, pronouncing us fit enough to be deported. Yossel remained angry at Doctor Lemberg for months, especially because the sons of three of Lemberg's friends were not among the six hundred. I was more conflicted about him and more intrigued by the mixture of personal qualities of mind and spirit that he brought to a morally complex position. After the war, as I found out more about Doctor Lemberg I tried to imagine him making this choice or that with the knowledge that his decision probably meant life for someone and death for someone else.

The leaders of Jewish Councils [*Judenrats*] under German occupation were seldom admired in Poland, but Doctor Lemberg was the exception. His story is unlike those of Reb Mendel and Shlomo Zelichowski, both spiritually gifted men and both resolute in moral resolve. And yet he possessed another sort of gift and a rare one at that: the courage to make difficult decisions in an immoral universe and the ability to be just under almost impossible circumstances. To the very end, he was trusted by our community. To many in Zdunska Wola, including my mother and father, he was heroic.

"Why did he do it?" I asked Father in the summer of 1940. "Why did he allow himself to be chosen as the Judenälteste? Why collaborate with the enemy in this way?" I was thinking of our cousin Srulik Gerszonowicz, who as a ghetto policeman was now carrying out the orders of the Germans against us. I was also thinking of Pick, who had been appointed the head of the Jewish police. I could think of few people more unlike Doctor Lemberg. I wondered how, in fulfilling his duties as the leader of our community and its representative to the Germans, he could avoid becoming like our cousin and Pick.

"Lemberg came to talk with me when he faced the issue of whether or not to become Judenälteste," Father answered to my surprise. Although I knew that they respected each other, he and Doctor Lemberg were not particularly close. The conversation had taken place a week before the Jewish community had to inform the occupation forces of our choice for the Jewish Council and the Judenälteste. The decree gave us until the last day of 1939 and was unambiguous concerning the council's expected behavior: "It is the duty of the *Judenrat* through its chairman or his deputy to receive the orders of the German Administration. It is responsible for the conscientious carrying out of orders to their full extent. The directives it issues to carry out these German decrees must be obeyed by all Jews and Jewesses."

Neither my father nor Doctor Lemberg doubted that the leader of the council would live under the thumb of the Germans and probably fail in most attempts at mediation. Without power, without something truly valuable with which to bargain, no process of mediation could consistently be successful. "If you thought all this, why didn't you stop him?"

"I know, I know," my father responded:

> But the truth is that Doctor Lemberg really didn't want to become the Judenälteste. We reminded him that all his life he wanted to be president of the *kehilah* [Jewish community] and that he had never succeeded. Perhaps the time wasn't right back then, and perhaps now was the right time to be president of the equivalent body. Perhaps now he could do more good than he could have done before. He was fluent in German, and he knew the ways of the Germans. Everyone in town respected him, both Jews and non-Jews alike, and he did not wilt under pressure. Besides, no one else was as trustworthy as he. We all recognized that he would have to make sacrifices, but we also thought that this might be his destiny. Perhaps even he thought so.

That explanation sounded too much like one of Reb Mendel's stories that permitted a variety of interpretations and thus did not make as much sense to me then as it does now.

I don't know precisely when Doctor Lemberg had arrived in Zdunska Wola, but I believe that it was before I was born. I do know that in the election for minority representatives to the Polish Parliament in 1922 he worked on behalf of the Jewish bloc of our town. And I know that his work was highly valued. Yet he remained an outsider, regarded with caution even as he was being officially thanked. Perhaps because it was so small, my hometown suffered from interminable intrigues. Doctor Lemberg was a victim of some of them, and although he stood for election to the presidency of the kehilah various times he was always passed over in favor of someone from what was considered to be the "right" party.

My earliest memories of him have nothing to do with politics. In 1929 or 1930, when I was seven or eight, a typhoid epidemic broke out in town and our apartment building was quarantined. In our family, only my father and a sister remained well. I remember looking out a window to see Doctor Lemberg driving up to our building in his droshke, one of only four in Zdunska Wola privately owned by Jews, and entering our home, his black doctor's bag in one hand and a slender walking stick in the other. He always wore a pince-nez and Western clothes, and he had neither a beard nor earlocks. I remember the gentleness in his hands as he felt my forehead for my temperature and palpated my chest and back, but I also sensed in those hands a great firmness. He came day after day for what seemed an eternal recovery time. After the typhoid epidemic he became our family doctor, and I saw him for this or that illness all the days of my childhood.

Being somewhat secular and an active Zionist rather than orthodox or a Gerer Hasid, Doctor Lemberg came down on the minority side of most issues. Such differences may have kept him from being elected to the presidency of the kehilah, but they did not prevent him from becoming one of our most respected citizens. His talent in medicine, in addition to his kind and attentive personality, endeared him to all of us. People listened when he spoke, for his words, always well modulated and delivered with thoughtful care, sometimes surprised by their combination of eloquence and concision.

A month or two before the German invasion, the Polish army issued a call for medical personnel, and Doctor Lemberg volunteered. During the first week of the war his division was sent to southern Poland. Soon he was captured but somehow managed to make his way home. He told everyone that henceforth he would put all politics and activism behind him and dedicate himself only to medicine. But that was not to be. Soon, and repeatedly, he was thrust into the center of things, either by the Germans or by his fellow Jews.

In early November of that first fall under occupation, the Germans rounded up many of the town's adult males, including Doctor Lemberg, and took them to Sieradz, the county seat. There the Germans tortured them, killing four, before allowing the rest to return home. My father would have been among those taken—

Germans soldiers came looking for him—had it not been for an ethnic German named Schultz who had been his partner on patrol when they both volunteered for the civil guard before the war. Although Schultz had told the Germans where some Jews were to be found, he also helped to hide my father and a friend. Ethnic Germans in my hometown often behaved like this, and thus we could never be certain who was reliable or who was treacherous.

Early in December 1939, Doctor Lemberg received "Jerusalem Certificates" (entry visas for Palestine) for himself and his family. The community despaired on hearing the news, and members of the kehilah who earlier had prevented him from becoming president now came to him and begged him to stay. He was one of the few Jews able to deal with the Germans and thus the community's best hope for decent treatment during the occupation. How could he refuse them, especially since at this time no one thought the war would continue for too long? Certainly no one in our town anticipated the genocidal policies of the Germans. So he stayed. From that decision, it seemed logical and inevitable that he should accept the request to become the Judenälteste.

From Lodz, late in the fall of 1940, came the news that Jews in the section of Balut were not receiving packages of food that many in our town were sending to them. The Jewish Council asked Doctor Lemberg to go to Lodz to see if anything could be done. Perhaps Chaim Rumkowski, the Judenälteste there, would have some answers. In any event, our council wanted to know more precisely how Rumkowski had organized the ghetto.

When Doctor Lemberg arrived in Lodz, he was taken immediately to see Rumkowski and prevented from meeting with Zionists and others who disagreed with Rumkowski's methods. The two leaders spoke the entire night. Rumkowski told Doctor Lemberg that because the Germans wanted to kill all the Jews, he considered it his primary responsibility to try to save as many of them as possible, first by sending some on a journey that would most likely end in death and second by making the ghetto indispensable to the German war effort. In order to be an effective Judenälteste under these circumstances, he had to rule with an iron hand, for only by benevolent despotism could one prevent people from eating the flesh of their neighbors. "Benevolent despotism" was not an ugly term, Rumkowski added, for with it he could earn the Germans' respect and better serve the ghetto.

For much of the night Doctor Lemberg held his tongue. Finally, however, he told Rumkowski that such a path would lead to the abyss of slavery and annihilation and that he could not follow it. The rift that opened between the two leaders that night was unbridgeable, and they both knew it. In the morning Rumkowski told Doctor Lemberg that eventually he would have to come around to his viewpoint. Doctor Lemberg said that he would rather die first. If the good doctor persisted in that attitude, Rumkowski replied, he certainly would die, and sooner rather than later.

Back in Zdunska Wola, Doctor Lemberg told my father and others what had been said. Although he had to respect Rumkowski's efficiency in running the ghetto, he added, he could not agree with his methods, nor could he conceive of setting himself up as a dictator. He could not believe that Rumkowski had become such an egomaniac, for before the war he had worked with orphans and been involved in charitable organizations. For days some of us in Zdunska Wola talked about the meeting between Doctor Lemberg and Rumkowski. We invented dialogues between them. We speculated on what they ate and what Rumkowski's offices looked like. Most of all, we were proud of how Doctor Lemberg had behaved and what he had said.

Doctor Lemberg returned depressed from Lodz. He must have begun to understand then what the rest of us still did not want to comprehend. We kept thinking that the nightmare would soon be over, that it wouldn't get much worse, and that there was light at the end of the tunnel. We continued to believe that even as the Germans deepened the war and achieved victory after victory throughout 1940 and 1941. Despite what was happening before our very eyes, we clung to a myopic optimism. Even on the day my grandmother was taken in the fall of 1940 we looked for a silver lining. After she left, as my mother, my sister Guitel, and I were cleaning out her bureau we came across a pattern for a burial shroud and bits of cloth that seemed to have been discarded from the shroud itself. We couldn't find the shroud.

"Did Grandma take it with her?" I asked my mother.

"She must have."

"Then is she not coming back?"

"She must imagine that she is not," she answered, "but I hope that she will soon return to us."

Of course she never did. Doctor Lemberg was not responsible for the selection of Grandmother and the other old people, the first group deportation from Zdunska Wola, but that was probably one of the few selections in which he was not involved in some way. Such "wedding invitations," as they came to be known, were invitations for deportation, for work assignments, and even for the gallows.

I suppose that at first he believed some of the German propaganda about people being resettled for the purpose of work. He must have been taken in bit by bit, transformed with brutal efficiency from protector of his community to collaborator in its destruction. I have often tried to imagine when and how he realized the extent of his transformation. Even after he met with Rumkowski, he probably thought that he could save the community or succeed in substantially delaying its ruin. Perhaps the realization came during the months between the hangings of Purim and Shavuos. I do know exactly when he had enough, however, for the story circulated throughout the town. Survivors spoke of it for years.

Orders for the selection process usually came down in peremptory fashion. The time allowed for producing the requisite number of people was always too brief, and Doctor Lemberg at first succeeded in delaying this or that order by a little while. Once, however, when Hans Biebow, a former German businessman who was head of the ghetto administration of Lodz and in charge of the transports from the surrounding towns, was visiting Zdunska Wola, Doctor Lemberg suddenly ceased even appearing to cooperate. Ordered by Hans Biebow to produce a list of a thousand deportees for the next day, Doctor Lemberg responded that he would not. Ordered again, he said he could produce the entire list right then and there. Writing three names on a sheet of paper, he handed the sheet to Biebow. Reading the names of Doctor Lemberg, his wife, and their daughter, Biebow screamed at him that he would pay with his life for such insolence. Nothing happened right then, but the threat deepened the dread in which the community lived. It was Pick who produced the list of a thousand deportees.

The end came in August 1942. As they did so often, the Germans created a mirage to distract people, a small oasis of hope and happiness that encouraged them to believe in a better future. Early in the month, Doctor Lemberg had received permission to bring back a hundred men from the camps, people whom he said he needed for the ghetto's workshops. In the camps around Poznan, a hundred inmates from Zdunska Wola were selected and ordered to be prepared to go on a transport. Neither I nor Yossel were among the chosen, although Joseph Levitt and Moischele Schorr were, both of them eventually to survive the war. The group arrived in Zdunska Wola on August 16, 1942, after a five-hour train journey. Most had been away for more than a year. The ghetto rejoiced and celebrated Doctor Lemberg as a miracle-worker. Nine days later, hundreds of German soldiers and a death brigade of the SS entered town.

Hans Biebow personally supervised what happened next. He issued a command that all the Jews from the ghetto go to the cemetery. Here the details about my family become vague. I know that my father, mother, and sisters were still in Zdunska Wola, so they must have gone to the cemetery along with everyone else. At the cemetery gate, eyewitnesses say, old people were separated from their families and children from their parents and then put into trucks and taken away. My four younger sisters were probably torn from my parents and my two older sisters at this point. My family and all of Zdunska Wola's remaining Jews spent the night in the cemetery, guarded by fully armed soldiers.

Close to three thousand people greeted the dawn the next morning. The order then came down from Biebow: Kill all but 1,200. I have wondered about the precision of that figure. Was it to be attributed to the German bureaucratic obsession with detail? Was it the limit that the transport train could take in the time allotted? Was it all that the ghetto in Lodz could accommodate? I don't know if my family survived that massacre, but I do know that Doctor Lemberg, his wife, and his daughter did. At noon that day, the Gestapo hunted Doctor Lemberg down in the cemetery and took him to see Biebow.

Biebow made him an offer. Lemberg really should be killed on the spot, he said, for his prior insolence, but he could be forgiven if he promised to collaborate and help with the transport of the remaining Jews to Lodz. There he would have authority like that of Rumkowski, for Biebow had observed that the Jews trusted and respected Lemberg and that they obeyed him. They thought of him as the "great Jew." Lemberg replied that he was by training and temperament a physician. In the Lodz ghetto he wanted only to work as a physician again, he had no experience in working with the Gestapo. Hauptmann Fuchs, who was present at the time and described this encounter to others, pulled out his gun and pointed it at Lemberg's head, intending to kill him right then. Biebow stopped him, saying that he would give Lemberg until the next morning to think things over.

Leaving the office, Doctor Lemberg ran into Pick, who told him of Biebow's intention to kill him the next day. A train was departing for Lodz that afternoon with two hundred Jews, Pick told him. If Doctor Lemberg could leave on it in secret, Biebow might be too busy with other matters to pursue him the next day. I have sometimes asked myself why Pick, of all people, should have been the one to try to help Doctor Lemberg at that moment. But perhaps even he had a conscience, however deeply buried. Years before, Doctor Lemberg had saved his wife during the typhoid epidemic, and it is possible that Pick's gesture was a belated act of gratitude.

Doctor Lemberg agreed to the plan after being assured that his family would follow the next day. Within an hour, however, the community found out about Pick's arrangements, and many rushed to Doctor Lemberg, again pleading with him to remain. As long as he was their leader, they said, they had a chance to survive. As before, he decided to stay behind.

The next day, Doctor Lemberg accompanied his wife and daughter to the train. Before entering the freight car, witnesses say, he told his wife and daughter that he had to take care of something and would join them in five minutes. He turned from them as they were being ordered into the car, and when they next looked for him he was gone.

When Doctor Lemberg left his family, Biebow's men apparently escorted him to the officers' car. There, asked by Biebow if he had changed his mind about collaborating with the authorities in Lodz, Lemberg said that he had not. I have not been able to find out exactly what happened then. He may have been killed in the officers' car itself, or perhaps the SS took him away from the train station and executed him out of the sight and sound of the Zdunska Wola Jews so as to avoid a possible panic.

In 1947 Biebow stood before a Polish tribunal in Lodz, accused of war crimes. Tried and found guilty of having participated in the extermination of seventy thousand Jews in Lodz, of having killed a well-known attorney named Weiskopf, and of having murdered Dr. Yakov Lemberg, he was sentenced to death and executed.

PART THREE
IN THE CAMPS

My Brother's Keeper, Part 1

After three days and nights in that textile factory in Zdunska Wola, Yossel and I, along with six hundred other young men, were herded onto a train. Traveling slowly almost two hundred kilometers to the northeast, it eventually stopped at Poznan, where between twenty and twenty-five labor camps would be constructed. Yossel and I were to work in three: one was Yunikowo, another was the cemetery camp of St. Martin's, and the third was called Fürstenfelde (Princely Fields), a romantic name for a horrible place.

Leaving the train, we were ordered to form rows of five abreast and march ten or so kilometers to the outlying village of Yunikowo. There we were led to a deserted factory building of three floors surrounded by substantial grounds. We were lined up in the *appel-platz* (roll-call yard), counted, and recounted. Then each of us was given a number that we sewed on our clothes, the first of several numbers we were to wear. My brother's number was 4020 and mine was 4041, and that is how we were known to the authorities for as long as we were in that camp.

The camp at Yunikowo consisted at first only of that empty factory building. It had no electricity, no indoor toilets, no running water, no facilities for washing, and no heat. Outside, all we had was an outhouse and a pipe with perforations on the bottom so that several of us could wash at the same time. Inside, the Germans had outfitted the factory building only with *pritches* (wooden sleeping platforms).

For the first two days we were beaten continuously and without warning. We were beaten if we did not stand up fast enough or if we did not turn around fast enough or walk fast enough. "Schnell, schnell, schnell," we heard over and over. We were ordered to clean the yard countless times, even though not a scrap of paper or sliver of wood could be found anywhere on the swept dirt. We had been allowed to keep only a few things from our knapsacks, like a toothbrush and underwear. I don't remember how I managed to hide my tefillin, but I did. Each day we were given only a bowl of soup and a quarter loaf of bread. Within a week, this program of humiliation and degradation made us submissive.

That first camp was not the usual *arbeitslager* (labor camp) and it was not a *vernichtungslager* (death camp). It was more like a prison. Our guards were Polish. Only the head of the camp and the main engineer were German. That camp we mostly built from scratch. Yossel and I were on the work details that built the kitchen, the outhouses, and the sleeping quarters. We also built an auxiliary rail line to link Yunikowo with the main rail line in Poznan.

In October, after four months in Yunikowo, Yossel and I volunteered to work in St. Martin's Cemetery near the center of Poznan. We became members of the "Death Brigade" and eventually came to be known by other inmates as the "gold diggers." St. Martin's was really two cemeteries. The new one contained the more recent graves dating from the middle of the nineteenth century. In the old one were buried prominent Polish aristocrats, scientists, industrialists, and artists. Next to it was the Jewish section, which was equally old but much smaller. The German plan was to empty the old cemetery and build on the leveled field an exhibition area for commercial fairs. A Berlin company named Hans Pracht, Hoch- und Tiefbau (Above and Below-Ground Construction) was in charge of the work.

Of course, to call what we did "work" would be to give it an undeserved dignity. Under the watchful eyes of our Polish supervisors, we dug up graves and removed jewelry, rings, and gold fillings from the corpses. We also cleaned the caskets themselves. Those in good shape were taken away to be reused. The others we plundered for their steel or brass, for the Germans found a use for everything. If the headstones were relatively plain, we would crush them, turning them into gravel for pathways. The larger and more valuable statuary was first appraised by a professor of architecture or of fine arts from the University of Breslau. We heard that one statue by a well-known artist from Düsseldorf was worth well more than 150,000 German marks. It and all the other pieces designated as valuable were carted off in the direction of the *gauleiter's* (appointed governor's) headquarters, or, as we called it, "the palace."

The Germans in effect "sold" the bodies of the Polish corpses. Those families who could pay 2,500 German marks were allowed to reclaim their family members and keep the caskets for reburial in the new cemetery being built on the outskirts of town. The corpses also were reburied in an individual grave with a headstone. If the family came up with something but still less than 2,500 marks, the corpse would be reburied without the casket but in an individual grave with a marker. Corpses without relatives, or with relatives too poor to pay the fees the Germans demanded, were thrown into mass graves.

By the time Yossel and I joined the Death Brigade at St. Martin's, all of the graves in the Jewish cemetery had been emptied. I don't know what happened to the bodies. Jewish law requires *k'vod hameth* (the utmost respect for the dead). The greater and more spiritual the person, the greater the respect to be accorded. Scholars and holy men are to be treated with a special reverence. Because our main job in the cemetery was to remove and pulverize headstones, every moment in that work was morally painful to us, and we tried to show respect for the dead whenever possible. We considered it a significant victory to do something, however modest.

On one of our last days on this job we came upon the headstone of Rabbi Akiba Eiger, one of the great talmudists of Poland. I recognized the name immediately and told everyone in my group about him. Of course, the Germans didn't know who Rabbi Akiba Eiger was or care about his piety and learning. To them, all that mattered was the size of the headstone, for it would yield more gravel than the others. Yossel and I talked with Moishele Goldberg and his cousins, who were working in another part of the cemetery, about what we should do. Finally, we decided only to pretend to obey our orders to pulverize every part of the headstone. Then, while Moishele distracted the Polish supervisors, we would try to hide that part of the headstone on which Rabbi Akiba Eiger's name was chiseled until we could bury it properly and in secret in a corner of the Jewish cemetery. And that is what we did. Two days later, while Moishele distracted the Polish supervisors again, Yossel and I quietly recited the kaddish as we buried Rabbi Akiba Eiger's name.

At the main cemetery, we were divided into squads. Moishele Goldberg and his cousins, all from the town of Sieradz, not far from Zdunska Wola, formed one squad. In mine, Yossel took command as The Engineer, although he was almost two years younger than I. He would plan how to dig up this or that grave, what to do first and what second. Even here his talent for organization and practicality was recognized. Because I was one of the shortest workers, I would climb into the grave after the casket had been removed and examine the pit carefully for bones, jewelry, or other things that could be considered valuable. Once in a while another body would be beneath the casket, and it was my job to discover it. The Polish supervisors were convinced that we were finding gold, and they would frequently search us after we finished work.

One morning while we were working in the main cemetery, Moishele Goldberg came over and whispered that I should meet with him and his cousins that afternoon in a mausoleum, which he pointed out secretly. There was something they had to ask me, especially because I was a yeshiva student. At the appointed time, while the supervisors were in another part of the cemetery, I sneaked into the mausoleum.

"Isaac," said Moishele. "Do you remember how Joseph interprets dreams?"

"Of course," I answered.

"Well," he continued, "since you know Talmud better than any of us, perhaps you can tell us what my dream means. For several weeks I have had a dream that keeps repeating itself. My grandfather keeps telling me to dig. 'Where?' I ask him. 'In the back yard of the fiftieth house of the main street,' my grandfather says. 'Main Street? What Main Street?' I ask him. He just tells me again, 'You will find treasure there, on the main street. But you must dig long enough.' And then he walks away, up a long street full of empty houses on either side."

"Is that all?" I ask Moishele.

"Yes, that's all. Sometimes my grandfather and I are walking. Sometimes we're in the stiebel. But he keeps saying the same thing. And the dream always ends with him walking up that street of empty houses. What does the dream mean, Isaac?"

"Perhaps it is very simple," I said. "Perhaps it means just what it appears to mean. Let's test your dream. Let's dig up the fiftieth grave of the *hauptallee* (main street) of the cemetery."

"We already removed that casket," answered Moishele.

"Maybe you didn't dig deep enough," I said. "Let's try again."

And so, while his two cousins stood as lookouts, Moishele and I climbed down into that fiftieth grave and started digging beneath where the casket had lain. For half an hour we dug. We found nothing. Then, just as we were about to give up, my shovel struck something with a dull sound. We found a baby's cup covered by several layers of a linen cloth. Inside the cup were twenty-one gold coins of various sizes. The four of us felt extraordinarily rich. Right then and there we shook hands and agreed not to reveal our discovery to anyone. I felt that this was the right decision and did not let even Yossel know about the treasure. I did so in order to protect him. I managed to keep the gold coins a secret until late spring or summer of 1943, when, in Fürstenfelde, he finally learned the whole story.

Moishele, his two cousins, and I divided the coins. In two days I began to talk to a Polish guard who seemed more decent than the others. When I was convinced he could be trusted, I gave him one of my coins. In return, over the next three weeks he brought me seven loaves of bread. I shared the loaves with Yossel and with others in my squad. When they asked how it was possible to get loaves from the guard, I said only that there was someone on the outside who was trying to do a mitzvah. That answer did not convince anyone, but they all knew not to ask any more questions.

Those gold coins made me feel as rich as a Rothschild. I began to think of the future, for the bread helped stave off our emaciation. It was, of course, not easy to hide the coins from the Polish guards, the *lagerälteste* (camp elder), and the *kapos* (heads of labor brigades), for there were frequent searches. But I kept the coins a secret, and so did Moishele and his two cousins. I would have the gold coins until Birkenau.

As luck would have it, on another day I found a hundred German marks. Until then, neither Yossel nor I had been tested concerning the private pledge we had made to each other in the textile factory in Zdunska Wola. We watched out for each other, of course, from the moment we were deported, but neither of us had yet faced a real crisis. As it turned out, Yossel was the first to do so. What he did saved my life.

Months after our deportation, we were still wearing the clothing we wore when we left Zdunska Wola. There were rips and tears everywhere. One afternoon, during a rare off day, the kapos lined us up in the roll-call area. A large carton of used clothing had just arrived from another camp. Called out by our numbers, one by one we went to the long table and received a pair of pants and a shirt. The kapos made no attempt to try to fit the pants and shirts to us, knowing that we would trade around anyway. We were excited. I grabbed my new pants and was looking through the pockets when suddenly a fifty mark bill fell to the ground from the small watch pocket. I quickly put my foot over the bill. Feeling the lining of the pocket, my fingers traced the outline of another bill inside.

As unobtrusively as I could, I picked up the bill and put it in my own pocket. Keeping my head down, I let my eyes circle the grounds. Had anyone seen me? I thought I was safe until, out of the corner of my eye, I noticed Simon Frumer looking at me. A slight smile creased his face, and he came over immediately. Six feet tall, still thickly muscled, and by far the strongest man among us, he towered over me. He grabbed my arm and squeezed my biceps hard, until it hurt.

"I saw what happened, Isaac," he said. "Give me the money."

By that time I knew there had been two bills in the watch pocket, but I thought he didn't know that. I offered Frumer the fifty mark bill I had picked up from the ground. He said he wanted all the money, not just some of it. He also demanded to trade his pants for mine, which would fit him better than they did me. That was true enough. The pants he had received were small for him, and my pants were large and loose. I offered him the pants plus the fifty mark bill. Out of the corner of my eye, I could see Yossel watching. Other people were watching, too.

"Give me all the money," Frumer snarled, "or you will regret this."

"No," I said. "What I have said is my final offer." Stubbornness, one of my more enduring character traits, has gotten me into trouble all my life, and I was stubborn that day in St. Martin's. I expected that at most Frumer would beat me up and throw me to the ground and then I would give him the fifty marks and the pants. I was wrong. He did punch me twice, and he did throw me to the ground. Then he walked off angrily, straight to the corner of the barrack where the lagerälteste, Israel ("Srulik") Rosenfeld and his two kapos, Pinchas Potrzebowsky and Shlomo Schultz, had set up quarters. I went into our sleeping quarters, where Yossel and I hid the two bills in the lining of my feather pillow. Not three minutes passed before the two kapos came for me and marched me to the lagerälteste.

"I understand that you have received a present in the shipment of clothing," he said.

I denied it.

"The money belongs to the German Reich," he continued. "I demand that you give it to me, for it is the confiscated property of the Reich."

I could not believe that a Jew from my own hometown would behave this way toward me and give himself these airs. In addition to my stubbornness, my tongue has also often gotten me into trouble, and I said something that to this day I have regretted. "What makes you think," I asked, "that you are the legitimate heir of the German Reich?"

His face reddened, and he clenched his fists. "Stand at attention!" he shouted. And then he ordered Pinchas and Shlomo, who had been watching all this time, to search me thoroughly. They found nothing, of course.

"Where is the money?" he screamed. "If we don't find it you will pay with your life."

I told him that I had dropped the bills by accident when I went to the outhouse. Although he didn't believe me, he ordered Pinchas to go look. From where I stood, I saw him poke around in the muck with his whip. After the search turned up nothing, Lagerälteste Srulik locked me up in a small cagelike cubicle, about four feet on each side, which was in the loft above the kitchen. The ladder to the loft was removed. Smoke from the kitchen tore at my eyes and hurt my lungs. There I remained all afternoon and all night. During the night, Yossel and a friend managed to get some bread to me on a string and a little bit of water.

The next morning Lagerälteste Srulik came to the kitchen. Looking up at me, his hand loosely holding his whip on his right hip, he said, "If you do not return the property of the Reich, you will be taken tomorrow morning to the stadium and hanged. I have informed the *baumeister* (civil engineer) of this decision and he has agreed."

The baumeister was a German civilian and the engineer in charge of the Hans Pracht Company. Part of his responsibilities consisted of overseeing the work we did in the camp. To inform him was serious indeed, for it meant that knowledge of the incident was not confined to the inmates alone. Still, I could not believe that these three kapos, each of them from Zdunska Wola and well acquainted with my family, would turn me over to an executioner. I remained defiant.

"I have told you what happened to the bills," I said, "and I have nothing more to add to that."

With that response, Lagerälteste Srulik cursed, turned on his heel, and left. I did not see him again as the day wore on. No food or drink was brought to me. I began to have doubts about the wisdom of being so stubborn.

"Isaac," my father used to say, "bend a little. Remember what the rabbis say about the oak and the reed. In a storm the oak will break and the reed will not."

Perhaps, I thought, the kapos will actually carry out their threats. Perhaps I should bend a little, like the reed. Still, I continued silent.

That afternoon before the roll call, the two kapos, Pinchas and Shlomo, came to the kitchen, put up the ladder, and ordered me down. "You can go, Isaac," they said.

"What happened?"

"Your brother saved your life. He understood the seriousness of your crime. He talked with the lagerälteste for a long time and got him to promise to release you and not punish you any more. Yossel was very persuasive. He also gave the lagerälteste the two fifty mark bills from your pillow."

The next morning after roll call, we all watched as another inmate from another part of the camp, accused of stealing a pair of gold bridges from a corpse, marched out toward the stadium to be executed. We never saw him again. Lagerälteste Srulik kept his word, and I was not punished further by the kapos or by any other authorities. Two days after my release from the cubicle, I was working with Frumer in the cemetery, emptying a grave. For a while, neither of us said a word. Finally, I broke the silence. "Look, you idiot," I said, "see what you did? Because of that neither of us has anything."

Frumer then punched me several times and bloodied my nose, although not as badly as he could have. That same evening, as a gesture of reconciliation, we exchanged pants.

The story of the hundred marks became known all over camp, and it was to benefit me in a way that I could not have anticipated. Among the Polish supervisors were two women cooks who prepared the meals for the Polish workers. Their food was much better than ours. Of these two women, the younger one, who was rather attractive, now took pity on me. One day she called out loudly, "Hey, Stomarek. Come here" (*stomarek* is Polish for "one hundred marks"). Going up to her I saw that she had separated out some leftover food for me. She gestured toward it, and I took it. This she did repeatedly. "Hey, Stomarek," she would call. If I were not within earshot, she would call my brother up to her. In that way we got extra food, and I doubt that we would have made it through the two winters we spent in the Poznan camps without her help. The hundred marks helped us out after all.

Although Yossel was almost two years younger than I and although in the ghetto I had been very much the elder brother, in the camps he was stronger than I and usually wiser, for he knew how to get along with people better than I did. I would keep getting into trouble, and he would keep getting me out of it. By this time, much of our talk in the camps had become talk about survival. If we managed to survive but were separated, we promised each other that we would to try to make our way to Israel and meet at Aunt Fruma Tyger's home in Haifa, for she was prominent and would be easy to find. We asked ourselves if it was worth it to survive.

It was then I told Reb Mendel's story about the discussion, reported in the Talmud, between the disciples of Shamai and those of Hillel. The debate centered on whether it would have been better for man never to have been created, and it continued for two and a half years. In the end, the parties agreed that it would indeed have been better had man never been created, but because he had been it was necessary that he make the best of it and examine his actions. In a similar vein, we, too, thought that it might have been less painful for us to have been killed early in the war, as Reb Mendel had been. Because we hadn't been so "lucky," however, it was our duty to survive. This was the first of several stories or experiences that became like a spiritual slogan to me. "Survive, survive," they all taught.

The idea of survival sometimes even penetrated our work routines. The Germans, in forcing us to work rhythmically when we did things like unload trucks, would often order us to sing. And so we would chant in Yiddish, *Uberleben, uberleben* (survive, survive). Sometimes we would chant a phrase from a prayer. Seldom did the Germans understand our pronunciation of words that in German meant the same thing.

Yossel saved my life several times. My first serious beating in the camps occurred in St. Martin's. For several days, Yossel and I had been working in a fairly isolated portion of the cemetery, and we were not closely guarded. I found a beautiful watch in one of the graves and put it in my pocket. On the spur of the moment I sneaked out to a nearby farm, where I traded the watch for a small bag of potatoes. Hurrying back, I got into the cemetery without a supervisor noticing that I had been absent. As I was hiding the bag in some bushes behind a row of mausoleums, however, a kapo came up behind me. It was Pinchas Potrzebowsky.

"Where were you?" he asked me.

"I went to the toilet," I said.

"You're not telling the truth. I checked the toilets. And what do you have there?" he asked, gesturing toward the bag.

"Potatoes."

"How did you get them?"

"A woman came by the fence and said that her sack was too heavy, so she gave me some potatoes from it."

"Just like that?"

"Yeah, just like that. There are some good people still in the world, you know."

"I'll let you go this time," Pinchas said. "Give me half of those potatoes. And don't ever let me catch you doing something like this again."

I gave him the potatoes, and because I still had some left I felt good. Later that very day I actually did go to the toilets. When I came back I saw Pinchas again, this time with Shlomo Schultz.

They were not mean people by nature, although they were short-tempered. Both would survive the war.

"Where were you?"

"At the toilets," I said.

"Don't lie to us, Isaac," they said. "You're endangering everyone's life. If you continue to lie, you will hang."

My tongue again got the better of me. "I actually did go to the toilets. And if I hang, you will hang next to me."

Almost as if my words had kicked them into action, both of them rushed me and beat me with their fists and leather whips, leaving scars that lasted many years. They beat me until I lost consciousness. When I came to, I was flat on my back. I couldn't move. Other inmates then put me into the empty barrel that had contained that day's soup. It was there that Yossel, who had been in another part of the cemetery when the beating took place, found me at the end of the workday. I was wheeled back to the camp in that soup barrel, helped out, and half carried to our sleeping platform. There, Yossel rubbed my back and legs. He stayed up all night, dampening pieces of cloth to put on my cuts, welts, and bruises. The next morning Lagerälteste Srulik, in an uncharacteristic act of kindness, declared me to be officially "sick" and allowed me to lie on the platform for three days. As soon as Yossel returned from the cemetery each afternoon, he would sit with me and nurse me. He also managed to get an extra ration or two from the attractive Polish cook who liked us.

My brother seemed always to understand better than I how to deal with camp authorities, how to speak to Germans. He understood the value of yielding when necessary, of not appearing to be stubborn. He understood, as I had not, that he had no choice but to give the Germans the hundred marks I had hidden in my pillow, not because I had "stolen" the money or because it "belonged" to the Germans but because they had power over our lives. Yossel realized that my life was worth more than a hundred marks. Before the war, before the camps, I would have laughed at the absurdity of equating a human life with a sum of money, especially such a relatively small sum. The camps taught me not only that Yossel had been absolutely right in what he had done but that also in some circumstances a man's life might be worth no more than a loaf of bread. The instrument of that lesson was Jakob Sittner. We would learn it in Fürstenfelde, where we arrived after spending Passover in St. Martin's.

The Neuman family. Back row, left to right: Mindel, Isaac, Esther, Yossel, and Luba. Front row, left to right: Hannah Malka, Gittel, Rachel (mother), Mordecai (father), and baby Yachet.

Zdunska Wola, ca. 1936–37. Left to right: Aunt Mirele, Aunt Rosa, Uncle Abraham, and Aunt Bluma.

A copy of the German identification photo of one of Isaac Neuman's sisters, Esther.

The main railroad station of Zdunska Wola, which Reb Mendel saw inaugurated and where all the deportations took place.

At Bad Goisern, 1946.

The tuberculosis sanatorium at Berg-bei-Linz, 1947. Isaac Neuman is seated second from the right. Most are wearing hospital uniforms.

Isaac Neuman (left) and Selig Golem, 1948, Ebelsberg, near Linz, Austria, in the woods near the camp.

Leading a seder in the rehabilitation center, Ebelsberg.

Neuman's brother Fischel (left) and a friend. They had just returned from the war and met in Lodz.

Conversing with a guest after the inaguration ceremony, Rykerstrasse Synagogue, East Berlin, 1987.

Isaac Neuman, 1999, Washington, D.C.

The Neuman family today: David, Isaac, Eva, and Mark. (Storch Photographer)

TEN

Unleavened Bread

One February evening in 1943, after the final roll call of the day, Srulik Rosenfeld asked about fifteen of the fifty inmates of our barracks to meet with him quietly. Our group of fifty had been separated out from Yunikowo, and we now constituted an isolated and largely self-sufficient camp on the grounds of St. Martin's Cemetery. Yossel, as always, was skeptical of Srulik's motives. Why, he wondered to me, would Srulik ask for such a meeting? He never had before. Was he going to tell us that we were being transferred? Did he have news of our families in Zdunska Wola? Were we fifteen going to be selected for a special work detail? At least, I said, we should listen to what he had to say. And so, about 8:30 we joined the other invited inmates at the back of the barracks, where Srulik and his two kapos, his brother-in-law Pinchas Potrzebowsky and Shlomo Schultz, had their quarters.

"Hert sich tzu, brider (listen closely, brothers)," Srulik said, with an expression both solemn and joyous. Yossel and I exchanged glances. Srulik did not normally talk that way, much less since he had become lagerälteste many months before. He wielded considerable power over us and appeared to enjoy doing so. I think he became accustomed to an authoritarian style in the Polish army, in which he served for several years. Soon after the Germans invaded Poland, he was captured and interned in a prisoner of war camp. There he learned the German way of doing things, as he never tired of reminding us. We were all wary of his power. A critical report from him to German authorities could lead to serious and painful consequences. Srulik's power had created a gulf between him and all of us. Calling us "brothers" would not bridge that gulf, but it did catch our attention.

Srulik's next words surprised us even more. "We must observe what the Lord did for us when we came forth out of Egypt." Srulik, quoting Exodus? We all knew now what the meeting was about. Tension eased. Yossel and I smiled at each other. Noticing our smiles, Srulik paused and then spoke, hesitantly but with intensity:

> I am the lagerälteste. I am in charge of everything that goes on here, and I usually don't ask anyone for advice, but this is different. Some of you know more about the laws and customs of Passover than I do. And I am not a learned man. But I do know that we are going through a biblical experience. Our situation here is as serious as our people's enslavement in Egypt thousands of years ago. Only God knows how much longer we will be the prisoners of the Pharoh. In six weeks it will be Passover. If we lived at home, all of us would observe it in one way or another, even in the ghetto. I propose to you that we observe Passover right here in this camp, right under the noses of our "friends." Well?

Suddenly there before us, in the cold and close air of that February evening, floated Srulik's improbable proposition. We had expected neither the proposition nor the speech. He was not one to make speeches; it was usually his brother-in-law Pinchas Potrzebowsky who talked. Srulik's words had a peculiar ring, as if he had long been rehearsing them and had committed them to memory. Stunned, we looked at each other, all of us, in silence. Then everyone began to speak at once, as children do when they begin to play a new game.

A strong and skeptical voice separated itself from the rest. It belonged to Ziggi Domb, my immediate boss as the leader of the Death Brigade. He was used to ordering us around and to having his opinions respected. "How," he asked, "can we observe Passover without a Seder?"

"We will have a Seder," answered Srulik, "but to have one we need matzohs. I think that we should save one-quarter of our flour ration over the next six weeks. The soup will be thinner, but we will have our matzohs."

"We can't afford that," Ziggi countered, lowering his head so it sat in his shoulders like that of a bull ready to charge. I knew, for Ziggi had told me so several weeks earlier, that he suspected Srulik of skimming off some of the flour already. "Too many potatoes and carrots have turned rotten over the winter," Ziggi continued. "We need all the food we can get. The soup is watery enough as it is. And if the Germans find out that we thinned it, then they will thin it for good. If we can't eat we won't survive past the spring."

"Shut up," said Moishe the woodcutter, his voice strained and harsh. Not one among us, not even Srulik, had ever told Ziggi to shut up, and Moishe was among the mildest people in the camp. "You get extra bread rations anyway, so you won't have any trouble surviving. What gives you the right to deny us Passover simply because it doesn't mean much to you?"

Ziggi was strong, healthy, and handsome; few in St. Martin's Cemetery Camp liked him. The son of the madam of Zdunska Wola's main brothel, he had grown into a tough and cynical man who took care of his own needs and desires before he thought of anyone else's. When we were growing up, we were impressed only by his fists and his ability to curse in seven languages.

I have always remembered exactly how Ziggi responded to Moishe: "I am not trying to deny you Passover. I myself would like very much to observe it. I want to thumb my nose at these German bastards as much as any of you. I really *am* worried about our health. We are all weaker now than we were six months ago. But if you vote to observe Passover here in the cemetery, I will work as hard as anyone to make it happen."

We voted. It was unanimous, with only Ziggi abstaining. Then we sat there, each of us marveling at the magnitude of our decision and the difficulty of implementing it. How would we have a Seder plate, and what would we put on it? What would we use for the *zeroa* (roasted lamb bone), for *maror* (bitter herbs), for *karpas* (greens), and for *haroset* (mixed apples, nuts, and wine)? How were we going to keep everything secret from our Polish supervisors and from German authorities? What would we do about the German troops stationed at the other end of the cemetery who manned their watchtower twenty-four hours a day? Even if we were to get enough flour for the matzohs, how would we prepare our unleavened bread, much less bake it? We had none of the utensils needed for the Passover preparations.

Srulik seemed to have answers to all the objections and difficulties. Because we couldn't keep everything absolutely secret, he said, we would bribe Szevczik, our Polish supervisor, with the price of a whore, the only condition being that he should not bring her into camp during Passover. Szevczik's bribed indifference would give us sufficient protection, for he was not virulently anti-Semitic. Generally, he carried out orders from the Germans and tried not to anger them. If the Germans found out that he had authorized a Passover celebration, he would be severely punished. So we paid him only for looking the other way, deliberately not telling him why we wanted him to do that. He, for his part, was wise enough not to ask.

"Just where will we put all this flour that we're going to steal?"

asked Ziggi. "We can't leave it in the storeroom, for it is inventoried. And we can't hide it in our barracks, for it would be discovered during any search. You ought to have thought of that, Srulik."

"I have," Srulik answered. "We will put the flour in Count Potocki's mausoleum at the entrance to the cemetery. It is large and has plenty of hidden storage space. No one will think twice on seeing us go in there. We can even dig a little grave for the flour and put a headstone over it." Srulik's humor, although lame, made me forget for just a moment how some weeks before he had almost turned me over to be hanged for not handing him the hundred marks I had found in a shipment of clothing.

The little joke loosened us up, and soon everyone was making suggestions. Before we knew it, we all had special assignments. My task was to help Yakov Koppel write down as much as we could remember from the Haggadah. Our difficulty, we discovered, was less in remembering the Haggadah than in finding a good enough pencil to use and suitable paper for what Yossel named "The Haggadah of St. Martin's," laughing at the incongruity. Yossel, too, had a special assignment. His engineering skills recognized as always, he was put in charge of the utensils. Somehow, out of the scraps of wood, tin, and stone that lay around the camp, he would manufacture whatever we needed.

The cold became less important to us over the next few days, and as soon as Szevczik agreed to the deal, we let the other inmates know our plans. We thought at first that no one would talk because there was no incentive in betraying us and to do so would mean going against the Polish supervisor and the lagerälteste. There was no danger in that. Everyone was so taken by the idea of observing Passover that no one thought of betrayal. No one talked to the Poles who had jobs in the other part of the cemetery or to the Polish cooks who staffed their kitchen. No one talked to the Poles who, contracted by the Pracht Construction Company, came in their horse-drawn wagons to the kitchen and delousing building every week and unloaded food supplies. Even Simon Frumer, whom no one had trusted since he had told Srulik Rosenfeld about my hundred marks, was brought on board, and even Simon kept his mouth shut.

What we thought at first would be the most difficult thing to accomplish, stealing the flour, turned out to be one of the easiest. Ziggi had challenged Srulik on effective thievery, and Srulik was up to the challenge. For the next six weeks, whenever we cooked soup for the noon meal the cook would skim off a cup of flour and put it in a paper bag, which he would then put in his pants pocket. At some time during the afternoon, he would walk to Count Potocki's mausoleum and leave the bag on the floor in an inside corner. Later, someone else would bury the flour in the "grave" Srulik had designated. After the first week, we began calling the flour the "royal treasure."

No German or Polish supervisor ever stopped the cook and searched him as he took the royal treasure to Count Potocki's mausoleum. That was likely due less to luck than to a general indifference, for we were usually left pretty much alone as long as we were docile and produced jewels and gravel from the cemetery. In that respect, as in several others, life in St. Martin's was not as difficult as in other camps. Looking back, I can't imagine being able to observe Passover, much less design and execute such a complex and secret plan, in the camps through which I was later to pass: Auschwitz, Fünfteichen, Gross Rosen, Mauthausen, Wels, and Ebensee. Not only were they different in kind and in how they treated inmates but also in their supervision, which was intense and constant.

Little by little, the tiny extra grave for the royal treasure in Count Potocki's mausoleum was filled. One afternoon I went there just to look at it, after which Srulik scolded me for drawing unnecessary attention to that mausoleum. Little by little, we assembled the other ingredients. Earlier we had discovered a weed called *lebjoda* in Polish, which was edible yet bitter enough to serve as our maror. Eaten in large enough quantities, the weed was noxious, and several months before some of us had gotten sick from having made a soup flavored with handfuls of lebjoda, but the small amount that we planned to eat on Passover would be harmless. I had tasted the weed out of hunger when I worked in a shed and could sometimes cook myself something to eat. I didn't like the bitter taste, which meant that it was the perfect choice for maror. As for the wine for the blessing and for Elijah, each of us was on the lookout for empty bottles that had a few drops still in them. That was especially difficult. The Poles drank vodka and German soldiers drank beer, but only German officers drank wine. Wine bottles were thus rare and hard to find. Yet over the weeks we collected enough for perhaps one-eighth of a cup.

We improvised also with the greens and the apples and nuts. As for the roasted lamb bone, we persuaded a Polish worker to bring us a chicken bone from a nearby slaughterhouse. "You want a chicken bone without any meat on it?" asked the worker, astonished at such a request.

"You stupid Jews," I heard him tell Srulik when he brought the bone and received a modest tip. "No wonder you're in here." I couldn't hear what Srulik told him, but I noticed him muttering something to himself and shaking his head as he walked away.

Moishe the woodcutter was put in charge of gathering and cutting firewood for the intense fire required to heat the oven for the matzohs. Yankel the shoemaker scraped out the wax left over from various chapels and memorial stones, for we would need candles. A shoelace was cut up and made into wicks. Although tedious, gathering wax and making candles was probably the easiest job of all. Yossel wondered if it was kosher to use Christian wax in a Jewish ceremony. I told him that it was permissible to do so and explained how I had used the wax from Christian candles for my private Hanukkah celebration in the monastery in 1940, assuring him that the situations were similar.

Yossel and his helpers made a new rolling pin and also fashioned a roller studded with tiny nails for preparing the matzohs for baking without rising. He also made a flat wooden shovel for taking the matzohs in and out of the oven. When all the ingredients had been assembled, we met again to discuss how we were going to bake the matzohs. We decided not to try to use the kitchen. We could be discovered at any time by a Polish worker who might stumble upon us or by a German patrol that would want to know why we were cooking at an unaccustomed hour. More important, the kitchen had no oven. In fact, the only oven in the cemetery camp was the delousing oven, which was located in the same building as the kitchen but in a separate room.

"See?" Ziggi told Srulik, his face grim with satisfaction. "There is no way to do this right."

"The delousing oven will work fine," Srulik answered, "and it will be the perfect cover. Whole groups of us can go into the delousing room without drawing attention to ourselves. Anyway, I suggest that we wait for the actual baking until all the workers have gone home for the day."

"That's ridiculous," Ziggi countered. "How can we use the delousing oven that much without arousing suspicion?"

Srulik explained:

For the entire week before Passover, one of us supervisors, perhaps Shlomo, can complain to Szevczik about how dirty you all are with lice and other vermin. After three days he will lose his temper and report our filth to his boss at Hans Pracht. And then the good Herr Baumeister will order the entire camp to be deloused. Because there are so many of us, if we start the delousing the day before Passover we will still be going on the evening of Passover. We can do everything just like a regular delousing. As always, we can strip, we can tie up our clothes in bundles, we can put the bundles in the oven, and then we can sit naked on the benches and wait for the clothes to be sterilized. The only difference now will be that on Passover evening, while we sit in the delousing room, the oven will be baking matzohs in the rear part of the oven and delousing our clothes bundles in the front part. That way, anyone looking inside the oven would see only our bundles of clothes.

We all liked Srulik's idea—all of us, that is, except Ziggi, who objected again: "But then the Germans will see the flames from the chimney at night, or a passerby will see them, and they will want to investigate such a suspicious sight."

Ziggi's objections were annoying, but they also helped us clarify things and be more cautious. At this point a man named Leon, who came from Kracow and who had been in St. Martin's only four months, spoke up. "At the Jagelonian University," he said, "I was a lecturer in continental philosophy, and my German is impeccable. If you get me a civil guard uniform, I can put it on that night and stand guard at the entrance to the camp. If Poles or German patrols ask about the chimney flames, I can explain about the delousing order. But I need a uniform."

Finally, Yossel and I said to each other later that day, finally Leon was to be of some use. Even in camp, his head was in the clouds, and he seemed physically unable to do anything practical. He was always the clumsiest one at every task and the last to get anything done. Up to this point his learning had been almost totally useless to us. When I was called Yeshiva Boy, it was said with some affection; when he was called The Philosopher, the words were derisive.

I don't know how Srulik found Leon a uniform, I don't even know if it was Srulik who arranged for it, but a few days before Passover it suddenly appeared. Although it did not fit perfectly, it was close enough, especially in the dark. In the meantime, just as Ziggi had predicted, we were all becoming weaker. Those who were stronger now shared any extra food with the weaker ones. Even Ziggi and Frumer, ordinarily very selfish, helped others this time. When we praised their generosity, they merely answered "temporary insanity" and shrugged off the praise, but we could tell they were pleased. As Passover approached, however, we all felt a surge of energy.

The day arrived. As soon as the Polish day workers left the camp, we transported the royal treasure from Count Potocki's mausoleum to the kitchen. After the sun set, Leon donned his uniform and began lookout duty at the gate of the cemetery. Inside the kitchen and delousing building the oven was hot. The bakers kneaded the flour into dough, and the rollers rolled, working fast so the matzohs wouldn't rise. Everything in any particular batch—from the moment the water touched the flour and the kneading began to the end of the baking—had to be done in less than eighteen minutes. Longer than that and the bread would rise, making it unsuitable for Passover. The entire batch would have to be thrown out, and all the utensils scrubbed to remove any contamination from them. In the delousing area, I sat with a group of other inmates, all of us naked, waiting for the first batch of matzohs to be brought from the kitchen for baking.

"Here it comes," I said, elbowing Yakov Koppel, who was sitting next to me.

"Mazeltov," we all said to each other when the first batch slid into the oven. As soon as I was done with my so-called delousing, I joined the rollers and for the rest of the evening occupied myself with taking batches of matzohs to the delousing room and shoving them into the oven with the special flat wooden shovel that Yossel had made. He started out as a roller and helping me, but after a while he sat and watched, a smile spreading over his face. Looking at him, I realized that at that very moment we were both happy. "Master of the Universe," I said to myself, "what a strange creature you have made in man, that he can experience happiness in something like this camp."

While we were thus occupied inside, outside, by the entrance gate, a German patrol became curious about the flames shooting from the chimney at that odd hour of night and asked Leon what was going on.

"Oh, you know how dirty these Jews are," Leon said. "They have gotten so filthy that Herr Baumeister ordered the entire camp to be deloused. Of course, it is taking a long time. There is nothing to worry about. Everything's under control."

The German patrol seemed satisfied with that response and wandered off, back to their end of the cemetery. What Leon did not tell them was at that very moment Szevczik was fast asleep in his separate living quarters at the back of our barracks. Three of us had given Srulik a gold coin each from that treasure hoard we had found in one of the graves. With that gold, a bottle of vodka had been procured for Szevczik. A habitual drunkard, he was unable to ration the alcohol and had proceeded to drink himself into a stupor. He probably wouldn't awaken until morning, but to ease our minds we stationed someone in the hallway that connected his apartment to our barracks to give the alarm should Szevczik return to consciousness and decide to leave the comfort of his bed.

It was close to midnight before all the matzohs had been baked and sorted. The fifteen of us on kitchen duty took all the plates and cups we could carry and silently walked from the kitchen and delousing building to the barracks. There everyone sat on the wooden platforms, not saying anything and not moving. Some were smiling. Leon may have looked incongruous in his civil guard uniform, but now he was respected by everyone. Every person in the barracks was handed an entire matzoh and part of another.

Srulik wanted to lead us through the Haggadah but didn't know it well enough, so he turned to the most learned of the inmates, Yakov Koppel, and asked him to begin the ceremony. Yakov stood up and spoke a blessing over the candle. Then he said kiddush and, reading from the Haggadah he and I had written, asked us to repeat with him: "Praised be Thou, O Lord our God, King of the Universe, who kept us in life and sustained us and enabled us to reach this season." Out of the corner of my eye, I saw Leon start, apparently surprised at the timeliness and relevance of the words. The next day I learned that it had been his first Seder in years.

Next Yakov dipped a bit of grass in water, blessing it as a symbol of springtime and renewal. It wasn't parsley, but it would do. Uncovering the plate of matzohs, he broke the middle matzoh for *afikomon* (dessert), to be ritually hidden at some point during the meal. Raising the plate, he asked us to repeat with him: "Matzohs symbolize the bread of our affliction in Egypt. May all who are hungry eat with us and celebrate Pesach. May all who are now slaves be free next year."

Next it was Pinyele's turn to speak, for he was the youngest, being younger than Yossel by about four months. Sitting on the edge of the platform, Pinyele asked solemnly, "Why is this night different from all other nights?" And so, now one of us, now another taking a role, we went through as much of the Haggadah as Yakov and I had been able to reconstruct. Every so often someone would say, "No that's not right. This is what should be said now," and we would accommodate that opinion. Little by little, we went through the story of pharaoh and slavery, of escape, of hardship, and of freedom. Every so often someone would comment, "Just as we are suffering here," "Just as we are hungry here," or "Just as we are slaves here."

The light from the two kerosene lanterns kept the room dim and cast our faces into half shadows, softening the lines of hunger and pain so evident during the day. I watched Yossel as his eyes became luminous and sad, and I knew he was thinking of our Seders at home. This year our sister Luba would have asked the four questions, and our father, as usual, would have led us through the Haggadah with the spiritual passion I saw only in people like Reb Mendel, Shlomo Zelichowski, and the Strykower rebbe.

Our voices choked as we proceeded. Pinyele did find the afikomon and without difficulty, and for this he was rewarded with an extra matza. Yakov put some drops of our wine into a cup for Elijah, asking us to repeat with him, "Elijah will come in answer to our prayer for help, and he will herald the coming of the Messiah. The world will then know peace and freedom."

I almost cried as we spoke these words and so did Ziggi, tough, cynical Ziggi. Leon's face now glowed with spirituality. Then Srulik took the Haggadah from Yakov and recited, closing the Seder: "We have completed the observance of the passover in accord with the law. Just as we have merited it in the past, may we merit it in the future and bring the pascal lamb as a sacrifice."

Despite all Srulik had done during the past six weeks, the words sounded odd in his mouth, as though he did not have the right to speak them. Others must have felt as I did, for, without anyone saying anything, the mood broke. Suddenly, the Seder was over. Pinyele, who had been crying for some minutes, dried his tears. All of us hurried to put away every scrap of evidence that suggested that a Seder had taken place. By morning everything had to look normal. The entire event had taken no more than half an hour.

Although we never talked about it with each other or told other inmates about our Seder, I believe that the simple meal of unleavened bread in St. Martin's Cemetery helped us endure some of our hardship in future camps. As time passed after the war, the meal began to grow in my mind in significance and spiritual power. More than fifty years later, I can still see Yossel's face in the dim light—and Srulik's and Leon's and Yakov's and Pinyele's.

"Next year in Jerusalem!" we told each other, embracing with faith but with little hope. By Passover of 1944, Yossel and I would be in Fünfteichen, where all our hopes and dreams would be reduced to one only: *uberleben* (stay alive).

My Brother's Keeper, Part 2

Jakob Sittner was one of the best bakers in Zdunska-Wola, famous for the joy with which he baked the cholent for our Sabbath meal. Every Sabbath around noon, Yossel and I would be sent to his bakery. Returning home, walking through the streets, we saw other boys and girls who had been sent on similar errands, and the air of Zdunska Wola was redolent with the smell of hot cholent. At four-foot-seven, Sittner was so small as to be almost a dwarf. And yet that was not how people thought of him, for he had a reputation for kindness, generosity, and impeccable honesty. As Yossel and I were to learn, that honesty coupled with a stubborn adherence to the truth got him into trouble.

Sittner was with us in the first transport from Zdunska Wola, and it was in the camps that Yossel and I really came to know him. When we were moved from our first camps of Yunikowo and St. Martin's Cemetery to that of Fürstenfelde, Sittner, because of his honesty and his prior work as a baker, was entrusted with the storage and distribution of the bread rations. One morning, some weeks after he had been distributing bread without incident, we heard shouts coming from the building where Sittner worked. It was the Polish commandant of the camp, beating Sittner.

"What did you do with the loaf?" the commandant yelled. Apparently, the night before he had counted nineteen loaves of bread and in the morning he counted only eighteen. He accused Sittner of stealing the bread and ordered a search. Nothing was found.

"I've done nothing wrong. I have stolen nothing. You are mistaken. You have miscounted," Sittner repeated over and over. That protestation of innocence angered the commandant even more. He called for Sittner to be taken to Poznan, where the Gestapo interrogated him. If he cooperated and revealed the names of his collaborators in the theft, the Gestapo told him, he would receive a lighter sentence. Sittner insisted that he had nothing to reveal.

Brought back to our camp after a week of interrogation, Sittner told us what had happened. That should have been the end of it. But then something must have snapped inside him, for he attempted to escape. He got as far as the railroad tracks, where he fell from a moving freight train and was seriously injured. We wondered if he had been trying to commit suicide or if he just had an accident. We couldn't believe it when the Germans sent him to a hospital. That turn of events caused considerable debate among us. After about two months, during one of our roll calls, the Germans read us a statement that Sittner had been found guilty of acting against the authorities of the camp and of conspiring to enrich himself at the expense of the Reich. The sentence of death would be carried out as soon as Sittner could stand unaided.

A week later the Polish guards marched us to a clearing in the forest not far from the camp. Sittner arrived in the back of a long Mercedes. Pulling him out of the car, the German guards tied his hands behind his back and ordered him to step onto a chair that had been placed under a thick limb in the largest tree at the edge of the clearing. The limb was about twelve feet above the ground. They placed a noose around his neck and slung the rope over the limb. As Sittner stood there, looking at us with blank eyes and a frozen face, the German commandant read out his crimes and sentence in a loud voice. At the end he stated, "The sentence has the full agreement of the committee of inmates of the Fürstenfelde camp."

With that, a German guard kicked the chair out from under Sittner, and we watched him jerk until he was still. Then the Germans ordered us to form a single file, to walk slowly around the tree, and to look at Sittner's body. Two of my companions requested of our Polish guards something that we never would have asked of our German captors: that we be allowed to give Sittner a Jewish burial. Nervously glancing to see if the Germans had noticed this conversation, the Polish guards whispered that such a request could not possibly be honored. Then we were marched back to camp. From that moment on, we all lived in fear of being accused of the smallest irregularity.

"See?" Yossel reminded me. "Do you understand now why I had to give the hundred marks to them back in St. Martin's? The truth is not important to them. Honesty isn't, either. They want to be obeyed. And they will do what they think they have to in order to get our blind obedience."

I agreed with him. "It may be necessary to act like an obedient slave here. And it may have been necessary to give up the money. You did save my life, Yossel, when you did that. But how do you think we have been getting extra food rations from time to time all these months? Why do you think we have been treated with some consideration in our work assignments?"

I then told him about the gold coins and explained that I had kept their existence a secret from him in order to protect him. Although Yossel was shaken at this confession, he was also grateful, and he began to understand that our ways of trying to survive the camps complemented rather than contradicted each other. Because of our personalities and talents, we could indeed be each other's keeper. We were stronger as a pair than individually.

In retrospect, Fürstenfelde was our best camp. We usually had more to eat than we did in other camps, either before or after. The Poles, not the Germans, were our supervisors. Although the work was hard, for we were building a railroad, Yossel and I were physically up to the challenges of the day. Through it all, however, a sense of doom hung over us. Part of that was due to Sittner's execution. But part was also due to a German Jew who had arrived in the camp shortly after we did. He worked as a technical assistant to the baumeister. "You've seen nothing yet," he kept telling us. "Soon you'll see real hell."

We tried in our minds to dismiss his talk as yet one more example of the doomsday pessimism that some of our companions in Fürstenfelde fell into that summer of 1943. But our pessimist was right.

In August, heavily armed SS troops arrived in Fürstenfelde and herded us onto a train of many long boxcars. Suddenly, a fear greater than any we had known, greater even than that of the first week in Yunikowo, possessed us all. The SS locked us into solid boxcars that had only one vent for air in the roof and two minuscule barred windows way above our heads. Over the next three days and nights we would hoist someone up every so often so that he could look out and tell the rest of us what he saw. Slowly, stopping often, we rolled through a scarred landscape of open mine pits, chimneys, smoke, fire, and ashen skies. The SS had placed an open barrel in the boxcar to collect our excrement and urine. Within half a day it overflowed. It was emptied only at widely spaced intervals, and I can still smell its stench in the summer heat. We stood face to face, back to back, thigh to thigh. It was very difficult to sit and virtually impossible to lie down. Every few hours we would try to make some room for one or two older or infirm inmates who needed the rest that a bit of extra space briefly provided. The watering stations where we stopped always had water for the train and the guards but seldom for us. Then we arrived in hell.

As the train pulled in, we heard the barking of dogs and shouted orders: "Los, los, mach schnell." German soldiers came among us, hitting left and right, and we sensed right then that this place would be different from all other places. At that moment, snatches of a melody from Reb Nachman of Bratslav came to my mind. Inwardly, I began humming it. That calmed me somewhat.

Auschwitz. Neither Yossel nor I had even suspected that such a place could exist. Barking dogs. Big Germans in heavy coats. Loaded weapons. Search lights, shouts, commands, whips. Clashing with the cacophony of our arrival in hell, the strains of Bach and Mozart from the camp inmate orchestra floated eerily through the station and processing rooms. This, I soon learned, was standard operating procedure. The music alternated between German classical pieces, Viennese operettas, and Strauss waltzes.

We were separated into two groups. The Germans commanded our group to remove our clothes and keep only our eyeglasses and shoes. We were sprayed for lice and shaved. Then we were lined up in order to be assigned numbers. I watched as the attendant, holding the electric needle in his hand, placed it over my forearm and in a swift series of strokes, as if he were stitching a bit of cloth, etched 143945 into my arm. I interpreted this procedure as a good sign, for the numbers burned into our flesh meant that we were not going to be killed immediately.

Despite being naked and pushed this way and that by the Germans, I managed to smuggle the gold coins into Auschwitz. In my hand was a piece of freshly baked bread that the Germans had given us and weren't paying attention to. When I sensed that we would be searched for valuables, I pressed the gold coins into the warm bread and then kneaded it around them. Once we had finished being processed and had gotten some clothes, I transferred the gold coins to a handkerchief and ate the bread.

I also managed to smuggle my tefillin into the camp. After being processed in Auschwitz, we were marched the two and a half kilometers or so to Birkenau. Before entering the gate and afraid that we would be searched again, I took advantage of a distraction to approach the fence that separated the inside of the camp from our area. I threw the tefillin into the tall grass on the other side of the fence, where they lay undetected until I recovered them two days later. Esther, I said to myself, you are with me still.

I lost the tefillin a few weeks later but cannot remember how. I do remember how we lost the gold coins, though. The day after we arrived, Yossel and I saw that we would have a better chance of surviving Auschwitz-Birkenau if one of us worked in the kitchens. We agreed to try to bribe someone on the kitchen staff with a gold coin to give me kitchen work. I gave the handkerchief with the coins to Yossel for safekeeping while I went off to speak to people in the kitchen. I didn't take any coins with me because they would probably be stolen from me if the kitchen staff thought that I had them on my person.

By the time I approached the kitchen staff, it was known that a number of the inmates from the Fürstenfelde camp had dug up graves in the cemetery at St. Martin's. I believed that our reputation as "gold diggers" would help in my negotiations in the kitchen. At the very moment that I was trying to bribe my way into kitchen duty, however, Yossel was losing the coins. As he was walking around the barracks, an older and larger inmate picked a fight with him. I think that he wanted Yossel's pants. During the fight, the handkerchief with the gold coins fell out of Yossel's pocket and spilled open. Several inmates saw the coins, and within ten seconds the coins had disappeared.

I didn't get the kitchen job. And the loss of the coins meant that both Yossel and I were under constant surveillance by the other inmates as well as by the kapos. We knew that we had to get out of this camp before something terrible happened to us. Our enemies were not only the Germans; we were afraid of the kapos, the blockälteste, and the informers. We were also being broken down by the four or five hours of sleep a night, starvation rations, the viciousness of the kapos, the constant roll calls, and even the prohibitions against talking or laughing. Somehow, in our other camps, despite everything, we were still human. Here starvation and death permeated even the air we breathed. We realized that few inmates in our situation lasted more than three months.

Thus, when representatives of the Krupp Munitions Works came to the camp and asked for metalworkers, both Yossel and I volunteered even though neither of us had seen a lathe machine or knew anything about metalwork. As the gates of Auschwitz-Birkenau closed behind us, I remembered the words of a learned Cabalist only three days earlier. Seeing the number on my forearm—143945—he gripped it and said, "Fire will never touch that arm." I hadn't noticed until he pointed it out that the numbers added up to twenty-six, which in the Kabbalah is the numerical equivalent of the ineffable name of God.

This particular factory of Krupp Munitions Works had just been relocated to Fünfteichen, about 150 kilometers northeast of Auschwitz. When we arrived at Fünfteichen, the camp was still being built and so we worked on that. At the Krupp factory Yossel and I were put in two different work groups. Yossel, far more skilled than I, was given a job that was technically more difficult and physically less demanding than mine. His job at the end of the production line for machine guns, in the quality control section, consisted of measuring and testing the completed weapons. Even some Germans worked alongside him. That was fortunate, for it meant an occasional extra piece of bread or a few cigarettes.

My job was on a different production line. I had to drill a hole in a piece of steel that was to become the butt of a cannon. I didn't mind the drudgery, for to be able to work like this was to be permitted to live.

One spring day in 1944, after we had been in Fünfteichen for several months, I wandered away from a group of inmates on a grounds-cleaning detail. I had noticed, in an untended part of the camp, what seemed to me to be new berries of some kind, and I decided to pick them. Maybe Yossel or one of the cooks would know how to make them palatable. I had barely gotten to the berries when I heard a shout, "Halt! Stehenbleiben!" So I stopped and slowly turned. A German guard was walking toward me angrily.

"What are you doing?" he barked.

I had seen some spring flowers a few feet beyond the berries, and so, in desperation, I replied that the commandant had asked me to pick some flowers for him. It was a lie, but I was in so much trouble already that such a lie could not possibly be worse than telling the truth.

"Why would he ask you?" snapped the guard. "What do you know about flowers?"

Necessity, they say, is the mother of invention, and my need was immense. Remembering that earlier a clerk, in filling out my identification papers, had mistakenly put "gardener" on the line for my occupation rather than on the line for my original address, which was Gardener Street, I blurted out, "I am in fact a gardener. It says so on my identification papers."

The guard checked, and my papers confirmed my claim. Luckily he didn't also check with the commandant to see if I had indeed been ordered to pick flowers. And that is how I officially became a gardener in Fünfteichen during my off-work hours. I picked flowers or aimlessly dug them up and replanted them elsewhere. I had no idea what I was doing, of course, but the Germans never seemed to find that out. The most important result of my newfound profession was that it kept me from being whipped or beaten as often.

By late fall of 1944, the soles of our shoes had worn through. Neither of us, we knew, would last through the winter without protection for our feet. Our situation was dire, for we had nothing with which to trade or bribe anyone, our gold coins having long since disappeared. We didn't know what to do until Yossel reminded me that in an unused corner of the factory stood some machines with leather conveyor belts. One afternoon when no one was looking, I cut a good piece of leather from one of the conveyor belts and wrapped it around my waist under my shirt. I thought that it would not be missed for one or two days. I was wrong.

On the march back to camp, just before we entered the gates, we were stopped. The guards ordered a thorough search for the missing conveyor belt piece and separated us into two groups. As soon as someone was searched and cleared, he was sent over to the second group. About halfway through the search, Yossel caught my eye and nodded. Turning around, moving away from me a bit, he then created a small diversion. I don't remember now what he did—something ordinary and almost inconsequential like stumbling, but it was just enough to get people's attention for two or three seconds. In those few seconds, I moved over into the second group and so escaped being searched. Back in camp, we cut up the conveyor belt and made soles for our shoes. We had two or three strips left over that we traded for bread.

The assembly line at Fünfteichen worked with hot steel, and we had to be very careful. The danger was not only the molten steel; there were also many sharp slivers that were created as byproducts of the process. One day, one of those slivers penetrated the back of Yossel's hand, between the thumb and the forefinger. At first, we didn't pay too much attention to the wound.

We removed the sliver and cleaned it as best we could. But Yossel's hand became inflamed. Although the swelling was noticeable, it didn't seem serious, and Yossel tried to hide his hand from the authorities so they wouldn't know that it was interfering with his work.

Two weeks after the initial infection, we suddenly were transported to a camp named Gross Rosen. Rumors flew that the Germans were being defeated and that this was the beginning of the endgame. While all this lifted our spirits, it also worsened our present situation, for the Germans became even less interested in keeping any of us alive. After Gross Rosen, we were forced to go to Mauthausen, my brother's last camp. It was at Mauthausen that I received, from a man who never told me his last name, the gift that was to save my life.

I knew him only as Shmuel, and he had arrived in Fünfteichen in March of 1944, a German Jew from a town near Czechoslovakia. A bit over forty, he seemed older, although when he first came to Fünfteichen he was still relatively fit, for his work as a tailor had allowed him to stay indoors most of the day. Tailors at the time were being treated more like servants than slaves. I remember envying his air of serenity and quiet self-assurance, even in a place designed to strip all that away. I remember even envying his prisoner's clothes, which were well mended and had buttons that matched. He even had real shoelaces. Most of us had to improvise. I used to watch him and wonder about his self-possession. He never fought over a loaf of bread. He accepted whatever was given to him without complaining. He was among the first to get up in the morning. I never heard him yell or swear or even show anger toward the kapos or the guards.

After our first conversations about family and the kind of life we had both left behind, we began discussing Torah. As I often did in order to find out how good a person's Hebrew was, I asked him if he could read the French rabbinic scholar Rashi. Because Rashi's script was somewhat different than the ordinary Hebrew, it was likely that those people who could read Rashi had received an excellent education.

"Yes," said Shmuel, "I can read Rashi."

And so began our intense conversations about Torah. Although I knew more than he did about the material, my book learning was complemented by his experience, and I enjoyed learning from him. By the time we were transported from Fünfteichen, I considered him my friend. Shmuel tried to help both Yossel and me during this time. I remember that he gave Yossel a pair of shoelaces just before we left Fünfteichen.

It was the cold of Gross Rosen, I think, and the lack of food that finally began to kill all three of us. Yossel continued to be the strongest, although his hand wouldn't heal; I was somewhere in between, for I was still recovering from a severe beating; and Shmuel, we could tell, was beginning to wear out.

Just as suddenly as we were forced to leave Fünfteichen, so were we forced to leave Gross Rosen. This time we left on foot, before dawn, in a biting and bitter wind. Our shoes cracked the snow's jagged crust. With whips and guns and shouts, the Germans marched us for countless hours toward Mauthausen. Those who fell and could not get up were shot. Yossel and I tried to support Shmuel between us, for we had begun to see the shadow of death in the lines of his face. Then a train and boxcars. Then more marching. I cannot remember how long it took to get to Mauthausen from Gross Rosen.

We were not processed upon entering Mauthausen in late afternoon. There in the roll-call area, within sight of the barracks that would have afforded some protection from the wind and the cold, we were given some bread and cold water flavored with coffee grounds and ordered to lie down on the ground until the next morning. And so we pressed ourselves against the hard, unyielding earth, trying not to imagine what the night would bring. Both

Yossel and I were better prepared than most of the inmates, for before leaving Gross Rosen we had found some cement bags that we had cut up and put under our clothes as a barrier against the wind. The bags, which were also somewhat waterproof, separated us initially from the dampness. Still, I was afraid that my clothes would freeze and that I would freeze after that, for as soon as the sun set the temperature plummeted.

As we lay down, we heard Shmuel, who was lying next to me, begin to pray. We joined him in the evening prayers. When we had finished those, he went on and on. I asked him, dreading the answer, why he was praying so long.

"Don't you recognize the prayers, Isaac?" he asked. "I am reciting the *vidui*." Of course, I had known and recognized the death confession prayers, but I had not wanted to believe my ears. I had never heard Shmuel say them or speak in this way. "This is not a good sign," he went on. "Look at the ice on the ground. Look at the crematoria. We are less than fifty meters from them. The Germans intend for us to die tonight."

He watched me carefully as I absorbed this statement. I said nothing, but the fear must have shown on my face. Yossel also had heard Shmuel's words. He had on a thicker coat than I and an extra layer of cement bags. Mentally, I began to prepare myself for death. Then, quietly, with great tenderness, Shmuel pulled me close to him and said, "I want you to have my coat tonight, for I am going to die, even with this thick coat. My time has come. But you might live, for the coat has an extra lining."

"I can't take the coat from you," I answered.

"If you really don't want it," he replied, his voice soft and urgent, "then I will give it to another boy. But I want you to have it. It is you who must have it, for you have studied Torah. You have had great teachers. You must survive. You must live. You must remember me, as you must remember all of us. You have a duty, Isaac. It is to teach Torah and to help others to try to understand what has happened to us."

I did not take the coat from him, but neither did I protest when he placed it over my body. I remember him looking at my face a long time, then turning his back to me and resuming his prayers. I heard his voice for a while but could not make out the words. After a bit the words stopped. I heard his breathing. Then I fell asleep. In the morning, parts of Shmuel's body were frozen to the ground. Yossel and I were among the few who survived the night.

"I thought you were going to die," Yossel said to me as soon as he saw me open my eyes in the morning. "I thought that the beating you received in Gross Rosen had weakened you too much." He was referring to the time, three weeks earlier, that the Germans had tried to separate Yossel and me by ordering us into different work groups. When I tried to get into Yossel's group, the kapo beat me with an axe handle until I lost consciousness. On entering Mauthausen, I still had bruises on my face and body.

Yossel's hand would not heal. We tried everything: hot soup, urine, ice. Nothing helped. Pus began to form under the skin, pushing it up and turning it purple, and it was spreading. Other inmates told us that he was getting blood poisoning and that without medical attention he would soon die.

That night, all night, Yossel and I talked. Not to go to the clinic was certain death. To go to the clinic was to take an enormous risk. To enter might mean never to come out again. To go to the door of the clinic and not be admitted might mean an even worse fate, for the Germans might kill Yossel as soon as they realized that he could not work in this condition.

"Please, Isaac," Yossel said to me. "You go first, and you get into line first, and then if they don't take you it won't be so bad because you can say you have a cold or an ache in your back and they will tell you to come back the next day. But if I go and don't get in, and if they see my hand, it will be my death sentence."

And so we took that awful chance. We had no other choice. I got into the line ten minutes before Yossel did. I gave the attendant my name and received a low number. Yossel took another and higher number and waited, and then, just before my number was called, Yossel exchanged places with me. Before crossing the threshold into the clinic, Yossel paused and turned around. His eye caught mine. He nodded and disappeared. He never came out. The clinic registry for Mauthausen on that day reads: "Isaac Neuman—died on March 21st, 1945. Cause unknown." Yossel carried my name with him into death. Part of me died with him. I saw little point in living anymore.

I was almost too numb to care, therefore, when the German troops again herded us onto another train. As before, the boxcars in their inhuman condition. As before, a slow, meandering journey. Once, while our train had pulled over to a siding in order to let a troop transport train pass, we were ordered to leave the boxcars to relieve ourselves. We had been out no more than three or four minutes when all of a sudden the Germans shouted, "Los, los, mach schnell." We rushed to climb back on the train. The man next to me, who had been defecating, was slow in getting his pants back on, and he stumbled a bit as he tried to catch up to me. I heard a German soldier curse at him and then I heard gunfire. The man dropped.

As I scrambled back onto the train, sneaking a look back at the still figure, I remembered Reb Nachman of Bratslav and thought to myself, "That could have been me. How can I not be afraid? The bridge is becoming more and more narrow, more treacherous, more impassable. So little separates one life from another."

Then we were pushed off the train and forced to march the rest of the way to Wels. Many died during this march. We weren't in Wels long. Then, as before, more boxcars, more forced marches. Many more died. We arrived in the Ebensee camp some time in April. I weakened rapidly. By the time the American troops liberated me and all my fellow prisoners on May 5, 1945, I was lying on the floor of the clinic in the Ebensee camp, barely conscious and unable to move. Later, doctors told me that I had been only a few hours from death.

Through the fog of those final days, I kept hearing Yossel's voice and Shmuel's in my head: "Remember me. Remember us." It was only that, and it was only the names that kept me from entering the eternal dark. Only the names. Hanania was there, and Poryia, Rabbi Akiba Eiger and Moishele, and Reb Mendel, and even Srulik and Pinchas and Shlomo, and Sittner and Jakob and Shmuel were there, and my mother and father, and Fischel and Guitel and Esther and Hannah Malka and Mindel and Luba, and Yachet, and most of all Yossel, my younger brother and my keeper Yossel.

PART FOUR

LEGACIES

TWELVE

Mottl's Torah

When I first met Mottl Chudi in the mid-1930s, I had no idea that someday his work as an artist and calligrapher would find a home in a synagogue in Israel or be sought after by a well-known museum. I never anticipated the many roads down which his artistic passion and talent would take him. I only knew I was fascinated by him. Although only five years separated us, that is a lifetime to a teenager, and Mottl seemed to be so mature and sophisticated. I admired his independence. Even in the 1930s, he no longer had side-curls and no longer wore Hasidic clothes.

Mottl grew up in Kolo, a small town about forty-five miles from Zdunska Wola. He had been sent to a yeshiva, and his family had great hopes that he would become a scholar or a scribe. But Mottl spent most of his time drawing. He drew on anything: cardboard, paper bags, and pieces of wood. He filled these spaces with still lives, gardens, and all the imagined cities he said he would visit someday. He also practiced calligraphy endlessly in Hebrew and Polish. One day when he was about fifteen, he suddenly quit the yeshiva and announced to his father that he was going to go to Paris to become an artist.

The announcement greatly upset his father, even though Mottl promised to return home after his Parisian training. Not only was he supposed to become the family's scholar, but there was also no future in Poland for an artist, especially a Jewish artist. "So, you want to study in Paris?" the father exploded. "Tell me, how are you going to eat? Who is going to pay your rent? Where are you going to live? Under bridges? Or perhaps you have a rich uncle in Paris?"

Mottl tried to explain, he later told me, that he was willing to do anything to become a good artist. That made his father even angrier. "So," he continued, "you would work in a restaurant as a waiter? How would you know what the people ordered? Are there any kosher restaurants in Paris? And how would you avoid eating eat pork and those crawling things from the sea? No son of mine will serve food in a treif restaurant. And what will you paint? Landscapes? Who buys landscapes? And God forbid that you should paint people. You know that the Second Commandment forbids that."

The fight was intense, and it lasted weeks. His father tried to change Mottl's mind this way and that. He begged him to return to the yeshiva or at least apprentice himself to a local scribe. But Mottl remained deaf to his father's words. At the end of the fight Mottl left home. He came to Zdunska Wola, where my grandmother took him in. Perhaps his father's entreaties had had some effect, however, for instead of going to Paris to study art he soon decided to study in Israel. In order to prepare himself for the journey, he went to live on a nearby *hakhshara* (collective farm) sponsored by a Zionist organization. The farm trained young men and women in the ways of a kibbutz and taught them the skills necessary to survive in the land of Israel.

Grandmother did not want Mottl to live on the farm. She asked him to stay with her and to let her fatten him up. He, as proud and independent as ever, refused, although he did promise to come to town on the Sabbath and during festivals. That was how I began to know him, and although he was too old to be an intimate friend, he did talk to me about his dreams and plans and we grew to like each other.

Those dreams and plans changed on the farm, for soon he met a girl there. Zillia was her name. They fell so in love that they had to marry at once. He was nineteen; she, eighteen. In about a year a son arrived, and Mottl had to put aside his burning ambition to become a great artist. Instead, violating the Second Commandment, he began to paint portraits of the local Polish gentry. While the family awaited emigration visas for Palestine, Mottl traveled from one marketplace to another, trying to sell his paintings. Despite his talent, he earned barely enough to put food on the table. Soon two more sons were born. There were three by the time the Germans invaded Poland. Three months later the entire family disappeared. Some people said that the Germans had taken him away because he had drawn caricatures of Hitler. Others said that Mottl could sense what was coming and had been smart enough to find an escape route. Most people thought that he had found a way to get to the Soviet Union.

No one heard anything of the family until after the war. Then one day in 1946 Mottl came to see me in a tuberculosis sanatorium in Goisern, Austria, where I was recuperating from my own ordeal. He was looking for Zillia and asked if I had seen her. I told him that I had not, and then we talked about our families, who had lived and who had died and how, if we knew.

His was a familiar enough story. I had heard and seen versions of it many times. He and his family were on their way to the Soviet Union when the Germans caught them and shipped them by train to a concentration camp. At the ramp of the railroad station, as he watched, the Germans separated Zillia first from him and then from their three young sons. She begged to be allowed to go with the children. She was ordered to take the other path, that is, the path that would allow her to remain among the living for a while. She refused. After some discussion, the commandant permitted her to go with her children. Mottl watched as they walked away and then watched as the Germans beat her into unconsciousness. Then he, too, was taken away. In a few weeks, she sent him a message from a nearby munitions factory of the camp that she was all right and then asked what he knew of their sons.

"Nothing," he sent back to her. "I know nothing." With that, both knew that the children had been killed.

After several months they were sent to different camps, and communication between them was impossible. Each had faith, however, that the other one was alive, and at the end of the war each one traveled from displaced persons camp to displaced persons camp, looking, looking. Always they seemed to miss each other, by weeks and even days at Ravensbruck, which was at that time in the British occupation zone. Finally, someone told him that she was in a displaced persons camp near my hospital, and so Mottl came to Austria. That's how he found me. But she was not in that camp, and I could not tell Mottl where she was. The trail went cold. Mottl gave up.

In one of our talks just before he left for Palestine, I asked how he had managed to survive. I heard the usual stories of persistence and luck, but he also told me that the commandant at the camp at which he had spent two winters found out that he could draw. He was ordered to make portraits of all the officers as well as to draw up architectural plans for this or that. Mottl's talent thus kept him indoors during the harshest months, and for weeks on end he was not beaten or whipped. "What would my father have said," he commented, "if he had known that my useless talent as an artist probably saved my life?"

So Mottl went to Palestine. As luck would have it, Zillia also went to Palestine a few days later. They met purely by chance at a grocery store in Haifa. She fainted. He brought her water. When she came to, they talked about their children. She could not accept that they were gone. For weeks she cried, and nothing could console her. Mottl, meanwhile, found a job as an orderly at the Maimonides Hospital in Haifa and had began to do calligraphy again. Now he used his talents for drawing up *ketubot* (marriage contracts).

Although Zillia kept busy through her work in a nearby hotel, she seemed to be sinking into an irremediable depression. Desperate about her health, Mottl decided that they should both visit a Hasidic rebbe who had emigrated to Haifa from Strykow, which was near Zdunska Wola, and was famous for his wisdom. He listened to them for hours.

When they finally fell silent, the rebbe said, "Mottl, you are an artist, a calligrapher. You should begin to write a Sefer Torah (Torah scroll) in honor of your children. Every stroke shall be dedicated to their memory. And you, Zillia, you, too, are an artist with your weaving and sewing. I charge you to walk the same path with Mottl and to undertake the task of weaving a mantle for Mottl's Torah."

Immediately upon their return to Haifa, Zillia went to the store to buy the appropriate needles and various colors of silk. She began to design the Torah mantle. When she showed her design to Mottl he accepted it without any changes, for it was beautiful. They began to work on their Torah and mantle together, and only together. Their time was limited, for Mottl had to be at the hospital at five in the morning and did not come home until the evening. Zillia had to be at the hotel at seven in the morning. She, too, worked a long day. After the dishes had been cleared away in the evenings, Mottl prayed and then spread the parchment over the carefully dried kitchen table. Letter by letter, line by line, the Torah grew. From her chair in the living room, as she watched Mottl bent over his parchment, Zillia patiently worked on the Torah mantle. Every year they saw the rebbe from Strykow and reported their progress. He smiled and quietly urged them to continue.

When I first visited Israel in 1959, I called on Mottl and Zillia in Haifa. By this time Mottl was almost done with the book of Deuteronomy. Zillia said that she was now stitching in their sons' names. After dinner, Mottl went to the corner store for some additional sweets. In his absence Zillia confessed a secret, asking me never to tell Mottl. She had almost finished her Torah mantle years ago, she said, but in order not to finish before Mottl she unraveled some of her stitching each night after he had gone to bed. Mottl's task, she added, was so much more important that hers, and it was much more complicated.

I saw Mottl and Zillia again in 1965. By now their eyes had cleared. They could smile. They were at peace. The Torah and its mantle had been completed. "Where is it?" I asked them. "I would like to see it."

"We gave it to the Fisherman's Stiebel in Haifa," they said. I learned that evening that a famous museum had offered Mottl a great deal of money for his Torah, for its beauty was legendary, but he had declined the offer. A year before my second visit in 1965, they had donated the Torah to the small synagogue in the harbor area, which they had attended for many years. The day Mottl's Torah was handed over was declared a city holiday. Mottl and Zillia were made *mokir-Haifa* (honorary citizens of Haifa), and the Strykower rebbe came from Tel Aviv. A parade was held in honor of the Torah, and it was marched from Mottl's and Zillia's home to the stiebel.

As luck would have it, a wealthy acquaintance from America landed in Israel from New York the very morning of the parade. He was on his way to an important meeting in Haifa. As a big donor for the past ten years, he was being honored for his charitable giving. His, however, was a self-congratulatory generosity that many considered offensive. As he entered Haifa, he found his way blocked by the odd parade headed by Mottl, Zillia, and the rebbe. Hundreds of people marched behind them, singing and dancing.

"What is happening?" the rich man asked an elderly policeman who had prevented his car from crossing the street. On being told, he fumed, "Why should I have to wait for the Torah of a poor hospital orderly to be paraded to a museum? I have an important meeting to attend, and I have given more in charity in one year than this poor orderly has in his entire life."

The elderly policeman, who like everyone else in Haifa well knew the years of love and labor that had gone into the making of the Torah and its mantle, ordered the rich American Jew back in his car. "Please wait until the parade is over," he told the American. "The Torah of this poor orderly counts for more than your meetings or your money."

Mottl's Torah, with its mantle by Zillia, is in the Fisherman's Stiebel still. I saw it there on another visit. And, if I remember correctly, Mottl is buried in a section of the Haifa cemetery reserved for Israel's martyrs and military heroes. And Zillia? I believe that she lives on in the same little house where she and Mottl created their Torah and its mantle.

THIRTEEN

Rachel

In 1935 the autocratic yet benevolent ruler of Poland, Marshall Josef Pilsudski, died. The whole country went into deep mourning, but those who mourned his loss the most may have been the Jews. Marshall Pilsudski was very friendly to us, and he also tightly controled radicals from both the right and the left. Fear and trembling seized the Jewish leadership because none of the rumored successors was considered sympathetic to minorities. Some candidates were even openly anti-Semitic. Poland's economic hardships fueled anti-Semitic propaganda and attacks on Jewish communities. The anti-Semitic press singled out prominent manufacturers and community leaders. Everyone in my hometown became worried. No one knew what to do. A number of Hasidim took their worries to the *alte* (old) rebbe of Strykow, the grandfather of the Strykower rebbe who in Israel many years later would guide Mottl and his wife in the making of the Torah scroll.

Instead of reassuring his followers and bestowing blessings on them, the rebbe himself seemed to be in doubt. Of course, he

In memory of my mother, Rachel Tyger Neuman.

prayed daily for the storm to pass, but each week things either got worse or at least got no better. At last he consulted with his family and with various prominent Hasidim and decided to make a special pilgrimage to Israel in order to pray at the western wall. If his prayers were not being heard in Poland, the rebbe thought, maybe God would listen to him at the holiest place in Jerusalem. His followers worried about him, however, for he was in his sixties and doctors had cautioned against such a long and arduous journey. But the rebbe felt that he had no choice. His was an appeal of last resort.

He was gone from Simchas Torah (mid-October) until shortly before the Hanukkah holidays. When he returned to Zgierz, many Hasidim from various parts of western Poland made a special pilgrimage to welcome him home and bask in the radiance of his face as he spoke of the Holy City. I saw him on Shabbat Hanukkah, and although I was too young to understand the deeper significance of the things he said, I well remember his words. During those holidays he spoke at each of the three meals: Friday night, Saturday afternoon, and the third Sabbath meal. Then again, after the Havdalah and the lighting of the Hanukkah menorah, he spoke once more.

My father and I listened to him together, and later I was to wonder just how far and how accurately the rebbe could see into the future. Each time the rebbe spoke on these holidays, the same subjects were further polished by his particular kind of musing, which we all knew and loved as *gematria* (meditations on words that speculate on their numerical values). Using gematria, the rebbe returned over and over to the themes of the Temple of Jerusalem, the western wall, and Rachel. First he pointed out the gematria of the word *Shabbat* (Sabbath). Its letters translated, he said, into the year 5702 (1941–42 of the Common Era), which he said was not going to be experienced as a Sabbath—or peace—by the world. He then used gematria on the same root, but with an additional *h*. The word he analyzed was *shovtah* (rested) as the word appears in Deuteronomy. The *h* represents 5. Adding that number to 1941–42 results in 1946–47. That would be the year, he said, when the earth would experience a sabbath. Now we know, of course, of the peace that was finally achieved in 1945 and of the birth pangs of Israel in 1947 with the U.N. resolution for partition. But in 1935 we had no concept of what was to come. Did he know what was going to happen? If so, why he didn't tell us, his faithful Hasidim?

After manipulating the word *shovtah* through gematria, he then pointed out the acronym for the song "T'nu Shira Vashevach La'ael Asher Shabath Barah (Give song and praise to God, who created the Sabbath)," saying that its acronym pointed to the year 5736—1975–76 of the Common Era. All the Hasidim who listened to the alte rebbe during those Hanukkah holidays were deeply disturbed and astonished. The rebbe in effect predicted that the years between 1935 and 1975 were going to be as difficult and as painful for Jews as are the birth pangs of a woman in labor.

Concerned about the sadness he saw on our faces, he said gently, "I have also visited the tombstone of our mother Rachel, and she still is our advocate; she is still pleading with the Almighty for our redemption." Later during Hanukkah, he would expand on those words in a way that to this day I have not forgotten.

On Saturday at the noon meal, he told us, "I saw the wall; I heard it crying. I touched it with the tips of my fingers and felt its tears rolling down." As he said this, his face became wet and ridged by pain. His eyes shone with an intensity I had not seen before. He assured us all that he had taken our *kvitlech* (written private petitions to the Almighty) and placed them in the crevices of the western wall. Even though I had not yet gone to Jerusalem, at that very moment I could see the wall, hear it crying, and feel its coolness.

To drive away the sadness, a most unusual mood for a Sabbath at the rebbe's table, the young men began to sing "Soll Schon

Sein, die Geulah (Let there be redemption)" and "Moscheiach Kummt Schon Bald (The Messiah will come soon)." Several of the Hasidim began to dance in a circle. The pace increased, and their voices became louder and louder: "Sheyibanhe beth hamikdash bimhera beyamenu bekarov (May the Temple be rebuilt speedily in our own days)." Most of the others joined the first group, but the rebbe and his two sons remained at the table, silent, with their eyes directed downward. Everyone could feel the tension in the air, and soon the dancing and singing stopped. On this Sabbath of Hanukkah they had expected the rebbe to talk, as he used to, of the miracles that happened so long ago and that were soon to be repeated. Instead, the rebbe remained depressed. Some attributed that depression to the long journey by boat and train and to his age. Others thought that he was ill and in pain. But everyone hoped that by the third Sabbath meal he would pull himself together and, as he often did, talk about the dedication of the Third Temple, which was bound to occur very soon.

The third meal came. Pieces of challah, herring, and *tsimes* (boiled and lightly seasoned carrots) were passed around. Again the rebbe went back to his earlier themes, but now he focused on Rachel. He had spent an evening at her tomb, he said, and was there at midnight, praying. We all knew that according to the Cabalists midnight is a particularly propitious time for mystical insight and experience. It is known as Tikun Rachel and Tikun Leah. If, the rebbe said, the prayers were recited with kavannah and with *hitlahavut* (fervor or ecstasy), they just might be effective in summoning Rachel. Citing the Midrash, the rebbe recalled how Rachel, in a time of dark despair for the children of Israel, had been asked by them to intercede with God on their behalf. She had come before the Holy One, blessed be he, and said:

> Master of the Universe, you know that your servant Jacob loved me with an extraordinary love. You know that he labored for me seven years, and when those seven years were finished and the

time had come for me to be married to my beloved, my father ordered me to trade places with my older sister. This was extremely difficult for me to do, but I controlled myself and had compassion for Leah. I knew that she must not suffer the shame of a younger sister marrying first. So I obeyed my father's order and handed over to Leah all the code words of our love between Jacob and me. I did so in order that, on the marriage night, Jacob would think that he was making love to me. I even hid under the marriage bed, and when he spoke to her in that night of love, I answered, and all so that he would believe that it was Leah he was loving and not me. I was generous with my sister. I prevented her from being shamed. And I was not jealous. And yet you, the everliving, eternal king, the all powerful one, the merciful one, you were jealous of idols. And because of your jealousy you have exiled my children, and they have been slaughtered with the sword, for you have permitted their enemies to do with them whatever they want.

The Holy One, blessed be he, listened to Rachel, and immediately his heart became compassionate. He answered her, as is written in the Book of Jeremiah: "Restrain your voice, Rachel, from weeping and your eyes from tears! For your labor shall have its reward. Your children shall return from the enemy's land. There is hope for your future: your children shall return to their own land."

The alte rebbe's voice grew soft and vibrant as he spoke further. "At midnight, after my prayer at her grave, Rachel herself appeared before me. She whispered in my ear, 'Do not worry too much, rebbe, I have a solemn promise from the Holy One, blessed be he, that my children will return to the land. Tell your followers that I will continue to be their advocate.' And I thanked Rachel, and then, with her by my side, I prayed 'Veleyereushalayim ircha berachamim tashuv' (into Jerusalem your city, you will return in great mercy)."

The room was silent. The rebbe had spoken of visions before, but never like this. And while he had spoken before of Rachel to his followers, this was the first time that he reported that she had directly transmitted to him a promise from God. In a deeply resonant voice, he said, "Rachel, of all the matriarchs, is most able both to appear before God *and* to move him to action. Rachel is our mother and our advocate. I cannot change the present or the future of Poland. But I can bring back to you from Israel God's promise to Rachel, which she whispered in my ear, that one day we would be returning to Jerusalem again. One day, we and our children and our children's children will be going home. Yet do not rejoice too much. For before that day comes, great darkness will descend on us."

He reminded us of the saying of a second-century talmudic scholar: "Let the Messiah come, but I do not want to be present." Would the times of darkness be so great, the alte rebbe said, explaining the words of the scholar, that even if the Messiah were to come the scholar would rather not have lived through those times? The rebbe continued, quoting Midrash, "When the holy temple in Jerusalem was in ruins, the Holy One, blessed be He, cried and said, 'Woe is me. Where are my children? And where is my sanctuary? Where are my priests? And where are my prophets?'"

That evening, as my father and I returned home, we did not speak. In the silence, though, each of us knew what the other was thinking. We were greatly comforted by the rebbe's words, but we were also deeply disturbed. We knew that the rebbe believed that enormous hardship and pain lay ahead for us. We could not imagine just how hard and how painful the road ahead would be before the earth would once again experience a Sabbath. We wondered if in our lifetimes it would indeed be true, as the rebbe said God promised Rachel, that we, her children, would be able to go home.

I was to think often of the alte rebbe and his story about Rachel in the years after 1939, when darkness descended on me, my family, and my community, as it did on Jews everywhere in Europe. And yet, although Rachel's words accompanied me from camp to camp and strengthened me in difficult times, I do not think of her mainly in connection with the Holocaust. That is because I was to hear her voice in 1987.

I had joined a group of American rabbis who were traveling together to Israel via Poland, Turkey, and Egypt. Of the eighty or so in the group, I was the only survivor, the only one who had actually come through the death camps. Two or three others had immigrated to the United States in the 1930s from Germany or Austria. Although it was not the first trip I would be making to Israel, it was the first time I would be returning to Auschwitz, and I chose to go with a group of rabbis because I could not bear the thought of going alone.

Even so, even in the company of colleagues, I began to tremble as we approached the main gate at Auschwitz, with its pathetic and hypocritical slogan about work making us free, "Arbeit macht frei." The very same gate, the very same words, and the very same railroad tracks. As I went through that gate I tried not to relive passing through them in 1943 and living here for a while as prisoner number 143945. Yet I could not help remembering how, by then, I no longer even had my original name, for the Germans had changed it for their convenience from Najman to Neuman. I also remembered how odd and foreign the German pronunciation of my name sounded whenever it instead of my number was used.

On entering Auschwitz in 1987, I first saw tourists. Tourists, I remember thinking, in a place like Auschwitz! Somehow that surprised me. And they were taking pictures—pictures!—like tourists everywhere. Even some of my rabbinical colleagues took out cameras and video equipment to record their visit, I suppose for their congregants back home. I tried to stay out of the range of their lenses. I did not want to become an exhibit, nor did I want to be put on display as "the rabbi who was there, a prisoner there, in 1943."

After seeing the mountains of hair, the mountains of tooth-brushes, and the mountains of combs, shoes, suitcases, and eye glasses, we walked the two or three kilometers from Auschwitz to Birkenau. We stopped at one of the destroyed crematoria, a crematorium dynamited at the end of the war not by Allied troops or airplanes but by four Jewish women inmates, and held a brief memorial service. We then walked over to a barracks that was still intact. It wasn't the barracks in which I had lived, but it felt so very familiar. I lay down on the first-level platform bunk. My bones remembered the wood, and in a minute or two they began to ache. I continued to lie there on my back, my body paralyzed by that wood. Two colleagues who had come into the barracks with me became restless.

"Isaac," they said, "are you going to lie there all day?"

"Isaac, why won't you get up?"

"Isaac, what are you doing?"

"Isaac, we're going to miss our bus."

"Isaac, please."

So I got up, and on the bus ride back to Auschwitz the memory of the hardness of the wood now mingled with the memory of the hardness of the wood then and with the pain, exhaustion, and the memory of the dulled sensibilities so necessary for survival. We stopped at one of the designated "Jewish blocks" and saw on display inside prewar Jewish placards, edicts by the German authorities in Poland from 1939, 1940, and 1941, as well as a variety of Jewish ritual objects and photographs of families. The rabbis asked me to say kaddish, so we put on our talesim and phylacteries and I led them in reciting the kaddish. Hardly had we finished when a rabbi from the East Coast took out his camera.

"Please," I asked him. "Not now, not here, not at this moment and in this place, and not me."

He put away the camera, but with reluctance. I did not have difficulty understanding that private citizens and ordinary tourists, Jews and non-Jews, might want to take pictures of such a place. But I did not understand how rabbis could visit a death camp and see it through the eyes of tourists. I thought of the words of the Holy One, blessed be he, "Where are my children? Where is my sanctuary? Where are my priests? Where are my prophets?" Oh Rachel, I asked myself, what happened to your promise to the alte rebbe?

From Poland we flew to Turkey and then to Egypt, visiting the thriving Jewish community in Constantinople and being shown in Cairo the progress Israel was making in restoring relations with former enemies. In Israel the planners of the trip seemed to be obsessed with filling every moment of our stay with importance. We saw the prime minister, the foreign minister, an important session in the Kneset, and, of course, the biblical sights. Fortunately, special care had been taken to secure guides who were extremely knowledgable in biblical lore.

Although we were grateful for the attention, most of us had tired by this time. Bus to bus to meeting to meeting to shrine to shrine—I was becoming exhausted by the scheduled business of it all. And yet, and yet. Without that tour I would never have come to the western wall at precisely that moment. Without that tour, I would never have heard Rachel's voice.

After a private two-hour visit to the archaeological excavations being undertaken then beneath the wall, we exited into the bright sunlight of mid-afternoon. The driver and the tour guide urged us to get back on the bus because there was one more important site to visit before the day was done, a site so important that I can no longer remember which one it was. Like diligent students, everyone obeyed, everyone, that is, except three of us. We wanted to pray at the wall. The driver and the tour guide asked if we knew our way back to the hotel, then shrugged their shoulders and left.

As we approached the wall for the second time that day, we all three were struck by a group of children who had just arrived from somewhere near Netanya. The teacher and their aides quickly and quietly arranged the children into rows and then into a circle. I especially remember the teacher, a small, vibrant woman in a kerchief, long blue skirt, plain blouse, and Yemenite jewelry. She led the twenty or so students, who must have been about ten, in the first liturgical prayer: "Veleyereushalayim ircha berachamim tashuv (Into Jerusalem your city, you will return in great mercy)." The prayer, I thought, the prayer of the alte rebbe. Then they began to sing, and with each song I knew I was where I belonged. I knew why I had come to Israel. Finally, faces illumined, light faces, dark faces, European and Yemenite, voices strong and clear, sabras and immigrants, they came to the final song: "Sheyiban-he beth hamikdash bimhera beyamenu bekarov (May the Temple be rebuilt speedily in our own days)." The same song, even the identical melody, to which the Hasidim sang and danced so many years ago.

The two choruses, the one in my memory, the other in my ears, blended. The years between the two songs vanished. Rachel's children had come home. I heard Rachel's voice in them. I began to cry. Suddenly, a gust of wind blew against the wall and wrenched a number of the kvitlech from their crannied resting places. Most fell to the ground. But one, lifted by the wind, flew over the wall and into the sky above. A private plea, I thought as I followed its flight, a private message brought closer to God by the song of Rachel's children, by her voice singing through them.

The rebbe's sadness of so many years ago contrasted with the hopeless dream of the Hasidim at his table, and they in turn contrasted with the impossible dream that now, in Israel and with Rachel's children, was near reality, near because the Temple itself had not been rebuilt and the Messiah had not yet come. But we were closer now, I thought, closer than we ever had been before, and I remembered the phrase "Atchalta d'Geulah (the beginning of redemption)." I whispered it to myself as we watched the children. We watched them until they left the plaza, and then we, too, left.

On the way back to the hotel, I thought of the Midrash concerning the destruction of the Second Temple in the first century of the Common Era. Four generals had been ordered by the Roman Empire to destroy that temple. Three had fully obeyed. The fourth general, who in the Midrash was identified as Arabic rather than Roman, left the western wall standing. Asked by his superior why he had not destroyed the final wall, he answered that it was important for future generations to know what a mighty civilization the Jews had built and that if everything were destroyed there would be no way to remember the power of the Roman Empire and its invincibility. And so, in the Midrash, the wall was spared as a monument to Rome's military power. Thus, according to the rabbis, it was an Arab who was responsible for preserving the central symbol of our home, the place to which all Jews, Rachel's children all, are drawn.

Yom Hashoah

"Remember me," Shmuel had said on the night he died at the entrance to Mauthausen on that frigid night in 1945, "remember us." But any thoughts of remembering or any sense that my memory might be significant were far from my mind in the summer of 1945. I was too ill. When American soldiers liberated me that May, I weighed perhaps seventy-five pounds. Tuberculosis racked my body. Years of starvation and abuse had given rise as well to other ailments. One night, as I learned from the nurse the next morning, I cried out in what the doctors thought was my death agony. She asked me what I had said, and I mumbled something about a promise to a friend that I would remember. That was the critical turning point, but although I was no longer dying I was also not yet living.

For the next eighteen months I lived in displaced persons' hospitals in Austria, first in Bad Goisern and then near Linz. My first doctors were German staff doctors working under American supervision, and I drew grim satisfaction from knowing that my killers had become my care-givers. During the first round of holidays and festivals in 1945 and 1946, from Rosh Hashanah to Yom

Kippur and Sukkos, from Hanukkah to Purim, Passover, and Sha-vuos, I alternated between anger and gratitude. I asked everyone I met for news of my family and friends, and I circled endlessly around questions of their fate. Gradually, I had to accept that except for my elder brother Fischel, who had fled to the Soviet Union during the early weeks of the war, all had been killed. I wrote to distant relatives in Sweden, and they responded with CARE packages and the news that Mottl Chudi was alive but that they didn't yet know anything about his wife.

As I began to believe that I actually would survive, I began to wonder: What now? How could I go on? What could I do? Recollecting Reb Mendel and Reb Nachman of Braslav's comment on the narrow bridge and the exhortation not to be afraid, I had to admit that I was afraid, terribly so. Now the fear felt different from that I had experienced during the war. I felt as though I were drifting on seas so altered by storms that no charts could guide me. The strange new world into which I was being reborn had little in common with the shtetl or with yeshivas, with the holy stillness of our Sabbaths, and with the quiet and luminous faith of Reb Mendel, Shlomo Zelichowski, and my father. I mourned the loss of my world and did not want to forget it. Yet remembering it was too painful, for the memory would be forever linked with how the Germans destroyed it. Now, healing yet not healing, I wanted to be released from the burden of memory.

From my hospital bed I received visitors from time to time. One day, the wife of Srulik Rosenfeld, the lagerälteste in St. Martin's who had mistreated Yossel and me, appeared at my bedside. A friend of Yossel came with her and stood a few feet off, shuffling his feet but saying nothing. She was afraid that I would denounce her husband, she sobbed. First she begged for my silence and then, when she saw I was listening, begged also for my silence about another kapo, Pinchas Potrzebowsky. I told her that although I would not denounce them, neither would I defend them if someone else denounced them and I were called as a witness. She sobbed her thank-yous, said that she knew how difficult it was to forgive a kapo, for she, too, had been in the camps, and then left. The next day, Pinchas, who would later move to Brazil and die there in the late 1950s, came to the hospital. Despite what I had told Srulik's wife, he was still anxious.

"How could you beat me like that over such a trivial thing?" I asked, reminding him of the bag of potatoes and how he and Shlomo Schultz had almost beaten me to death that afternoon in St. Martin's Camp. "We are both Jews. We are both from Zdunska Wola. You knew my family."

I've never forgotten his answer: "When you are high up, as in an airplane, the people below look like beetles. I was so high that you looked like nothing to me."

Two days after Pinchas's visit, it was Srulik's turn. Avoiding my eyes, he said, "You know why we did those things, Isaac. We did them only in order to survive."

After he left, I lay there, wondering, what price survival? What would Reb Mendel have made of this? Had they made the best of it? Had they examined their actions? Had I? Had anyone? I had no answers anymore.

In Linz, I continued to be very ill. One afternoon a group of American doctors examined all of us and decided to send the sickest to a sanatorium in Switzerland. I was not on the list. Wondering why, I got a friend to distract the station nurse while I sneaked into the records office and pulled my file. There I saw that the doctors thought that the journey would kill me. *Transportunfähig* (not fit to travel) I read. Somehow, the knowledge that I was sicker than the sickest among us liberated me. Anyone as sick as I had the right to enjoy whatever time was left. In a couple of weeks, at first in secret and without permission, I began to leave the hospital for day trips into town. I found the synagogue, or rather the part still standing, and began going there, at first to study and then to take part in the services.

At the synagogue, I ran into Joel Zolna, who had been with me in Mauthausen and Wels and whose successful escape I had helped plan in early 1945. Joel, it turned out, lived in an apartment on the old synagogue grounds. He had just married the daughter of the chair of the Jewish community of Linz. Now well-off financially, he began to invite me to his home as well as to restaurants, nightclubs, and concerts. Good food, good music, and good company gradually began to heal me. Massive doses of vitamins also helped, as did the books I began to read in the hospital library on history, philosophy, psychology, sociology, and medicine. After a number of weeks of attending services at the make-shift synagogue, I was asked to lead a service. After that I was certain I wanted to continue studying and wondered whether perhaps I could teach Judaism someday.

Over us all hovered the cries of the dead. Kaddish echoed always in our ears and often surprised us when we least expected to be reminded of death. Some who survived were dying. In the hospital room to my right an elderly Hungarian Jewish physician, dying of lung cancer and sedated by opium, would begin to wail as soon as the opium wore off. I listened to his frequent tirades for hours as he pounded on my wall and on the locked door to his room, moaning, "More opium, more opium." He took several months to die.

After being released from the hospital in the fall of 1947, I was moved to the special treatment unit (STU) of the displaced persons' camp in nearby Ebelsberg, Austria, where I continued outpatient treatment. In the next room lived an old Romanian alcoholic. I was given the responsibility of doling out a shot of whiskey for him each day. At seven every morning or before, he would bang on my door and demand his drink of the day. Once,

tired of his verbal abuse, I let him stand in the open doorway
while I held the bottle out the window and threatened to drop it
if he did not adopt more civil behavior. He gave me no more
difficulty after that.

I began to attend lectures at a local adult education institute
and to read more widely. My first steps toward a new life in America were so modest that at first I did not recognize how momentous they actually were. One afternoon I was introduced to a Mrs.
Pomeroy and a Mrs. Cadbury, members of an international commission sent by the United Nations to investigate the conditions
of people in the displaced persons' camps. I must have impressed
them favorably, for they designated me to be the liaison officer for
the camp. My job was to resolve disagreements among my fellow
inmates as well as mediate among us and representatives of the
United Nations and the American Jewish Joint Distribution Committee (AJJDC).

After several weeks of successful mediation, I began to think
that I might be able to do this for a living. It wasn't that different
from what the rebbe of Zgierz sometimes did. I even began to
dream of getting an education in America and starting a new life.
Becoming a rabbi was in the back of my mind, but it wasn't something I spoke about at the time. Somewhat to my surprise, the
staff of the JDC encouraged me to go to America, although they
immediately pointed out two great obstacles in the way. First,
although my tuberculosis was arrested, I was considered a health
risk, a problem the JDC solved by placing funds in an escrow account to care for me in America in the event my illness returned.
Second, I needed a sponsor. Sponsorship was difficult to obtain
without a profession or an officially recognized way of earning a
living. That problem was solved when I reminded the JDC of the
mistake of a clerk in one of my first camps. Instead of typing "Gardener" as the name of my street in Zdunska Wola, he had typed
"gardener" on the line that identified my profession. The clerical

error had once gotten me slightly better treatment in Fünf-teichen. Now it eased my admission to America under a special provision in the current immigration law that advocated preferential treatment for "agricultural workers."

That was how Isaac Neuman, gardener, although as ignorant of gardening as of nuclear physics, landed in New York on April 11, 1950. Behind me in Europe lay the shattered remnants of my culture and life. I had not been able to see my brother Fischel since the end of the war. In effect, I had no family. Even the brief love affair I had with a local girl in Linz had ended.

I arrived in New York with two letters of recommendation, the first from the area director of the JDC in Linz and the second from a welfare officer of JDC in the U.S. Zone. That second letter, by a woman named Jean Goldsmith, was addressed to Professor Pinchas Churgin of Yeshiva College in New York City. I made an appointment to see Professor Churgin, and in a few days, letter in hand and full of hope, I climbed the stairs to his office. Encouraged to believe he would help me and might even invite me to study at the rabbinical seminary of Yeshiva College, I was stunned by his indifference. I could not enter Yeshiva College without a high school diploma, the professor informed me, and I could not be accepted into a rabbinical school without a college degree. I had neither. My question about how to remedy those deficiencies was received with silence. Leaving his office that day, I walked the streets for hours, wondering what to do, where to turn to, whom to ask for help, and how to survive.

A couple of synagogues in the city offered me odd jobs, which I took until a job was advertised for an assistant—a janitor, really—at a synagogue in Miami. There, my luck began to turn, for Rabbi Joseph Narot befriended me. One day, after one of the many conversations with him in which he was obviously testing my knowledge, he told me that he had taken the liberty of writing to Hebrew Union College in Cincinnati on my behalf and that the admissions committee had agreed to interview me. He lent me money for a one-way airplane ticket to Cincinnati.

I had an unknown friend in Ohio, one of many I have had in my life, for on that admissions committee sat a former lieutenant in the U.S. Army who had participated in liberating the camps. This man, introduced to me as Dr. Katz, persuaded the rest of the committee that it should take a chance on me. Thus, I was provisionally admitted to rabbinical school, provided I could make up my academic deficiencies and obtain a bachelor of arts degree. Somehow the rules were bent again, for without even a high school diploma I was allowed to enroll as a special student of the liberal arts and humanities at the University of Cincinnati. A scholarship from the National Federation of Temple Sisterhoods was awarded to me, and that generous support continued through all my years of study.

The meandering academic journey upon which I then embarked suited me perfectly, although at times I seemed to be pursuing several careers simultaneously. Shortly after I began at the University of Cincinnati, I also began to study for a bachelor of Hebrew letters degree from Hebrew Union College. I had all but completed my studies for both degrees when I received an offer to become rabbi of the Kol Shearith Israel Synagogue in the Republic of Panama, and I served that synagogue between 1957 and 1959. Returning to America, married now to Ruth Cohen of Panama, I became rabbi of Temple Emanu-El of Dothan, Alabama, a position I held from 1959 to 1961. At the same time, I managed to finish my bachelor of Hebrew letters in 1958 and my bachelor of arts degree from Cincinnati in 1960. I received my rabbinical ordination from Hebrew Union College in 1960.

Life smoothed out, or appeared to smooth out, after 1961 when I followed a more conventional path by becoming rabbi at Temple Judah in Cedar Rapids, Iowa, where we stayed for the next thirteen years with our growing family. These were tumultuous times in America, however, both because of civil rights and the Vietnam War, and I did not withdraw from the fray. In Dothan I had been involved in civil rights, to the point that a fellow member of the clergy advised against endangering myself and my family. In Cedar Rapids I again became involved in integration and spoke at colleges and universities, both black and white. All that activity led to demonstrations in the Midwest and to the Selma march in Alabama, where I met Martin Luther King, Jr.

Whenever and wherever I spoke, I told audiences that if we Jews had been able to demonstrate from the vantage point of solidarity, and if the Christian world had joined us, the Holocaust might not have happened. I implored black Americans to learn from the Jewish experience.

At a black college in Fort Valley, Georgia, I urged students to become witnesses of their lives and struggle. They had a duty to remember the history through which they were living and speak about it, as well as a duty to commemorate their families, friends, and communities. I urged them to create their own Haggadah and so teach their children, as Jews do every Passover. I did not tell them about being urged by Shmuel in a similar way. Indeed, I told no one about that incident until working on this book, but the thought of Shmuel was with me on that afternoon in Georgia as it has been with me often.

Ruth and I sought close ties with the black community in Cedar Rapids and tried to bring up our sons in an integrated community. Instead of sending our son David to the most prestigious preschool in town, which was completely white, we sent him to St. Paul's Methodist Church, perhaps a strange thing for a rabbi's family to do, but we did so because it was integrated. When Martin Luther King, Jr., was assassinated in April 1968, I went immediately to the black church closest to my neighborhood to offer condolences and any help I could. David, who was seven at the time, remembers us being invited to the memorial service, and he remembers seeing his mother among the women upstairs, the only white woman to have been accorded such an honor. It was in Cedar Rapids that my marriage, my family, and my career first thrived. It was also in Cedar Rapids that my marriage fell apart, and Ruth and I divorced in 1970. She moved back to Panama, and with her consent our two sons remained with me. In 1974 I moved with them to Champaign, Illinois, to become rabbi of Sinai Temple. In both Cedar Rapids and in Champaign, I occasionally wrote stories or anecdotes in addition to my sermons. While an active rabbi in Champaign, I received an honorary doctorate from Hebrew Union College in 1985, and on May 5, 1986—the forty-first anniversary of my liberation—I was appointed to the U.S. Holocaust Memorial Council by Ronald Reagan.

In 1950, arriving in America, I experienced part of its special legacy to humankind and its generous and maternal embrace of newcomers. Because of an undying gratitude to my liberators and adopted country, I have often volunteered as an auxiliary chaplain to the Armed Forces, especially for Passover and Hanukkah, and have been sent overseas on several occasions. My affection for America has never been diminished, even when I disagree with the policies of its leaders. Even when I protested the Vietnam War, I was careful to state that I supported the Armed Forces, for I have always had the utmost respect for Americans in uniform. Nor was I protesting against a country, for I love America and what it represents and have come to consider the United States as my true home and think of myself as American as those whose families have been here for generations.

After retiring from Sinai Temple in June 1987, I served as rabbi of East Berlin and the German Democratic Republic, the first rabbi to work there since World War II. Why, I have often been asked, did I chose to return to the county that murdered my people? The answer is that I returned for the sake of the Jews and of Judaism. I believe it is a necessity and a duty to help other Jews in distress, wherever they may be.

I went to East Berlin in order to aid in the restoration of a small corner of Judaism. Soon, however, I ran into difficulty, and for gestures that in America would have turned no one's head. For example, I adopted the following lines of prayer from the Orthodox prayer book as part of the ritual of every service: "Our brothers and sisters who are in distress in foreign lands, may they come into freedom." Such a statement, even in the sparsely attended religious services of our marginalized group, was too revolutionary for East Berlin in 1987. The Stasi (East German secret police) identified me as a troublemaker and established a file on me. I was followed on my walks and on trips. Even private meetings with other people were spied upon. My telephone was tapped and my mail opened. Although I was provided with a car and a driver, the driver was a Stasi informer; the housekeeper, a charming and gracious woman, also informed on me.

I did not at first sufficiently appreciate that the main intention of the East German government was to use me and my efforts at restoring Judaism purely for propaganda purposes. They had promised to allow me to function in East Germany as I had functioned as a rabbi in the United States, with freedom of the pulpit, open access to periodicals and other publications, and freedom of movement. Almost immediately upon arrival, however, I was forbidden to say anything about Israel. Zionism was even more taboo. I wasn't granted the funds to undertake repairs to the synagogue or to heat the sanctuary properly. My periodicals, for example, the *Jerusalem Post, Time Magazine,* and *Der Spiegel,* were intercepted and delayed. Soon they stopped arriving altogether. Diplomatically worded complaints were to no avail, and after a while I began to acquaint foreign correspondents and visitors from the West with the real situation. Finally, discouraged by the entrenched resistance to everything I tried, I resigned in order to return to America.

My sojourn in East Berlin did have a long-lasting positive result, however, in that I established an adult education series that still continues. More important, I met Eva Grünstein, a professor of anthropology at Humboldt University, who became my wife in July 1988.

The Holocaust was the single greatest event of my life. There is no denying its influence on me, professionally and spiritually. But I have not lived completely under its shadow, and I have tried not to make it a burden for my family. I am sure that neither son can remember a time when he did not know I was a survivor. The tattooed number on my arm and my rabbinical activities ensured that. Moreover, they heard stories of the Holocaust and Polish Jewry from visitors to our home as prominent as Abraham Joshua Heschel, Elie Wiesel, and Viktor Frankl or as unknown as the cousins who lived in Florida and were wonderful storytellers. Yet neither the Holocaust nor my being a survivor were the most important realities of their lives. Rather, if asked, they would no doubt identify as most important their being the sons of the rabbi of the Jewish community in which they lived.

It is primarily through survivors like me that the Reb Mendels and Shlomo Zelichowskis of Central Europe have continued to live, and I feel a great duty to their memory. Whenever asked to speak in public on the Holocaust, I do not use figures. I don't believe that I have ever spoken in general about the "six million." Instead, I have spoken of individuals, of singular acts of courage, and of spirituality. It is important to me that people not forget how teachers like Reb Mendel taught, how the rebbe of Zgierz helped his followers, and how people in Zdunska Wola lived. That is not easy to get across, and I have felt sometimes as if I were a voice from a silenced song, a kind of echo sent here to remind others of the sound of Judaism.

Yom Hashoah (the remembrance of the Holocaust) has become a significant commemoration in Judaism, and I have tried always to make it both meaningful and aesthetically appealing. Many congregants have commented that our Yom Hashoah observances remind them of the memorial service on Yom Kippur afternoon, the Ne'ila. Perhaps all these years, I have been trying subconsciously to recreate the spiritual mood of the Ne'ila service that Shlomo Zelichowski observed on that fateful day in 1942 when he prepared himself and his friends for death. Yet there is a problem with the official act of remembrance. I do not believe that one can "remember" what one has not experienced. In that sense, most American Jews cannot remember the Holocaust. What I, as rabbi, have always tried to do, therefore, is to recreate images and scenes of a world that has been lost. I introduce Reb Mendel or Nochem Ellia Zilberberg or Doctor Lemberg or even my grandmother and through their stories try to preserve our Central European past.

I have attempted something similar with my sons, Mark and David. Mark, who had worked at the White House, was with me when Ronald Reagan inaugurated the cornerstone for the Holocaust Museum in Washington in September 1988, a project on which I had input. He was also with me for the inauguration of the museum itself in 1993. We walked through the exhibits together, lingering the longest at the one of a milk can that had been filled with documents and buried in the last days of the Warsaw ghetto. The documents in that rusted milk can, one of several discovered after the war, are the gold of our people. They bear witness; they are memories come alive, testimonies to Jewish spiritual resilience, resistance, and dignity. They demonstrate how, in the midst of destruction, starvation, and degradation, one can do scholarly and spiritual work. Warsaw's Jews remembered, as Jews have done for three thousand years, and tried to pass on something of their spiritual life and experiences. The modern Jewish community, in turn receiving that legacy, has an obligation to embrace it. "In each and every generation," the Haggadah says, "every individual should feel personally redeemed from *Mitzrayim* [bondage in Egypt]." Auschwitz is our Egypt. After World War II, everyone, gentiles or Jews, has a duty to try to imagine themselves going through Auschwitz and experiencing liberation.

In August 1994, David and I traveled to Poland, in part to see my old haunts. We flew into Warsaw from London. Early on, we decided not to visit any death camps, but both of us wanted to see Warsaw, Lodz, Zgierz, and Zdunska Wola. Although I had gone back to Poland after the war to visit my brother Fischel in Warsaw in 1956, I had been back to Zdunska Wola only one other time between 1956 and 1994. I was not surprised by what we saw. All signs of Judaism were gone from the streets, the buildings, and the town. Gone was our stiebel, the main synagogue, the Beis Midrash, and gone the plaza between them, gone the *mikvah* (ritual bath) of the community, the marketplace, and old town hall. I showed David where my grandmother's and father's store would have been if the town hall still existed. Also gone was the apartment building where my family had lived before Yossel and I were deported. A newer building stood in its place, with the look and feel of standard public row-housing of postwar Europe. As we faced that alien facade, I could feel David trying to imagine my old home. Walking through Zdunska Wola, I looked into every older face, searching for one who might be familiar, but every single person in Zdunska Wola remained a stranger.

From the site of our old apartment building, we drove to the Jewish cemetery. Its gate had been bolted shut, but we managed to borrow a handmade ladder from a Pole who lived next door and so climbed over the wall. Inside, most of the headstones, covered by the tall August grass, lay on their sides. We righted a few, brushed off the dirt, and read the Hebrew. Fifty-two years earlier, also in the month of August, several thousand people had been murdered in that cemetery. It was there that the rest of my family was destroyed and separated, parents from children, sibling from sibling, and husband from wife.

Leaving the cemetery, we took the car to Zgierz, where I tentatively pointed out the Rebbe's Court. Because we had followed the old trolley lines, I knew we were on the right street and the right block but could not identify the house itself. And so we returned to Warsaw, and then in a day or so we returned to London. Only shadows have remained to suggest Jewish life in Zgierz and Zdunska Wola. Here and there were a paving stone or a gravestone, a lock on a cemetery gate, old trolley tracks, or a face that because of its age had to have been there, had to have seen and experienced events I and others had gone through but from the other side.

I don't want my sons to feel paralyzed by the sadness, grief, or anger that goes with mourning a world destroyed by great evil. Over the years I have tried to teach them and other young people not to stand idly by and let injustice occur. Evil cannot be permitted to flourish. One must fight against it and convince others to do the same. When I see an innocent person suffer or someone weak or defenseless being taken advantage of, I am pained and try to do something about it. If I don't, I feel even worse.

Yet despite the evil of the Holocaust, it was the evil itself that also showed me the miracle of those individual acts of kindness and courage under the most difficult conditions, acts that renewed my faith in God and humanity. The light of my faith, although sometimes dimmed, was never extinguished. I survived not only through luck and persistence but also because here and there, in the midst of hell, someone cared for me. Someone gave me a piece of bread after a beating. Someone gave me his winter coat on a frigid night. Someone stretched out his hand.

Afterword

As far as memory, intention, and research permit, this book is true. Everything is based either on firsthand experience or on the verbal accounts of people who were there, on other written eyewitness accounts, and on the historical record. Some of the details stem from Isaac Neuman's conversations with other survivors after the war but before work on *The Narrow Bridge* began. That is the case especially for Joseph Levitt and Moischele Shor, known as Joe and Morrie after coming to America, who were both deported from Zdunska Wola some time after May 1941. Both were among the hundred men allowed to return to Zdunska Wola just before the final destruction of the ghetto in August 1942. Both survived the war, and both were helpful concerning events and people in Zdunska Wola between May 1941 and August 1942. Joe's wife Mina, who worked in a factory in Zdunska Wola alongside Mrs. Lemberg and knew the Lembergs fairly well, was also helpful.

Correspondence with Ester Freudmann in Sweden, a relative of Mottl Chudi, clarified some details about Mottl's life. Isaac Neuman's elder brother Fischel returned to Lodz for a while after 1945 before emigrating to America, where he would live for twenty-six more years. He contributed, as family members always do, to keeping specific memories alive. Aunt Fruma Tyger, who emigrated to Israel in the 1920s, was a font of information and anecdotes about the Neuman family and about Zdunska Wola until her death in the 1970s. Many people from Zdunska Wola visited her home in Haifa over the years.

Zdunska Wola was apparently considered so insignificant that it was not accorded a separate entry in the *Encyclopedia of the Holocaust,* an indication of how thin its historical record is. Nevertheless, general histories of the Holocaust have been perused, for example, those by Lucy Dawidowicz, Martin Gilbert, and Raul Hilberg. More specialized works on Poland have also been examined, for instance *Kiddush Hashem: Jewish Religious and Cultural Life in Poland during the Holocaust* by Rabbi Shimon Hubberband, *Chronicle of the Lodz Ghetto* by various individuals, *Auschwitz Chronicle* by Danuta Czech, and *Judenrat* by Isaiah Trunk. The most useful secondary work for *The Narrow Bridge* is *The Zdunska Wola Book,* published in 1968 by the Zdunska Wola Association in Israel. This "Memorial Book," which has a brief introduction in English, consists mostly of memoirs and eyewitness accounts of the Holocaust in Hebrew and in Yiddish. It served as a complement to memory and was useful for the evocation of a few signal events in Zdunska Wola after May of 1941.

Although this book is factually accurate, it is neither strictly a memoir nor a work of history. Rather, it is intended as a recreation of the lost world of Polish Jewry before and during World War II. An important component of that world is Hasidic, and the teaching of spiritual truths in Hasidism is most often accomplished through stories. These stories were written in the spirit of Reb Mendel and other Hasidic masters, who, steeped in the oral traditions of Judaism, have transmitted its culture to succeeding generations. Inspired by them, in honor of them, and in memory of those who died in the Holocaust, we have attempted to continue the transmission.

The Narrow Bridge is the product of concentrated collaborative work between 1994 and 1998. We finally came to conceive of our collaboration in the following manner: Isaac Neuman was responsible for the "soul" of the book. These are his stories and his experiences, his memories of conversations with his teachers and others, and his vision of Hasidism and life in Zdunska Wola before and during World War II. Michael Palencia-Roth was responsible for the "body" of the book. He wrote the first drafts of each chapter or section, basing those drafts on conversations with Isaac Neuman and on prior written versions of some of the events.* He also shaped the entire manuscript. Body and soul came together in the collaborative revisions that each chapter received until both coauthors were satisfied.

We gratefully acknowledge the help of the following people: Eva Grünstein Neuman and Elaine Fowler Palencia read or listened to every story and improved the manuscript substantially, and David Neuman and Mark Neuman contributed memories and suggestions. The mistakes that remain, be they of fact or of presentation, are our own.

*Three of the chapters depend on earlier stories by Isaac Neuman that appeared elsewhere. A shorter version of "Hanukkah in a Monastery" was published in *American Judaism* 13 (Winter 1963–64): 16, 47; and in *The Jewish People's Almanac* (New York: Doubleday, 1981), 184–86; and elsewhere. It also appeared as "Hanukkah in Hiding" in *Good Housekeeping* 207 (Dec. 1988): 60–61. An earlier version of "Shlomo's Last Prayer" appeared as "The Shofar's Last Sound" in *Jewish Spectator* 48 (Summer 1983): 14–17 and in German as "Des Schofars letzter Ton," in *Dialog mit Polen: Beiträge zur deutsch-polnischen Verständigung,* no. 7 (1988): 49–58. "Unleavened Bread" expands upon an article entitled "Celebrating Passover—In Concentration Camp," Champaign-Urbana *News Gazette,* March 31, 1991, E6.

Glossary

afikomon: a piece of matzoh hidden at the beginning of the Seder and
then searched for and eaten at the end of the evening

al Kiddush Hashem: "for the sake of sanctifying the name of God" (martyrdom)

Appel-platz: the roll-call area in a concentration camp

Arbeitslager: labor camp

baal t'kia: the shofar-blower

baal-tshuva: a penitent

Becher: wine goblet

Beis Midrash: study house

bekovid: respectable but not ostentatious

Berachot: first tractate of the Talmud dealing with prayers and blessings

Biedermeier: a style of interior decoration that makes a room appear comfortable and was popular with the middle class in the late nineteenth
century.

bimah: platform where the rabbi or the cantor stands

Blockälteste: the elder of a barracks, a concentration camp trustee

bubemayses: here used as "grandmother stories"

Cabalist: a scholar or expert in Jewish mysticism

challah: special braided white bread baked for the Sabbath

cheder: literally "room," here, a one-room elementary religious school

chevley leidah: birth pangs

cholent: a special dish (usually consisting of a mixture of potatoes, meat,
and kugel) taken to the baker on Friday and left simmering in the
oven there until Saturday noon

chumash cheder: intermediate school for beginners in the study of the
Pentateuch

chumash seuda: party in celebration of a five-year-old beginning the
study of the Pentateuch

dos pintele yid: the hidden spark of the core of one's Jewishness

Droshke: a small, hooded, horse-drawn carriage

echod: the One and only One

Emek-halacha: the name of a Talmudic Academy in Warsaw

Endecja: a nationalistic, anti-Semitic political party in Poland between
the wars

Erev Shavuos: the evening before Shavuos

gartel: prayer rope worn around the waist by Hasidic Jews

Gauleiter: a state governor appointed by Hitler

gematria: numerical equivalent of Hebrew letters used in mystical and
rabbinic lore

Groschen: penny, in Polish currency

Haftarah: prophetic texts read, recited, or chanted on Sabbaths and at
festivals

Haggadah: the narrative story of the Exodus recited at the Seder

hakhshara: preparatory training on a farm during the Diaspora for living
on a kibbutz in Israel

haroset: a symbolic Passover dish consisting of apples, figs, nuts, wine,
and other ingredients

Hashomer Hatsair: Zionist socialist youth organization

Hasid (Hasidim): followers of a religious movement founded by Israel Baal
Shem Tov (1700–60) that worships God with joy and ecstasy

Hauptallee: main street

Havdalah: special prayer recited at the end of the Sabbath and festivals

hitlahavut: fervent ecstasy during study and prayer

Jahrzeit: anniversary of the death of a beloved relative or friend

Judenrat: ghetto administrative board appointed by German occupation forces

Judenälteste: the elder or the chair of the Judenrat

Kabbalah: Jewish mystical tradition

kaddish: prayer of mourning recited toward the beginning and end of formal worship services

Kapo (Kapos): supervising head of a labor brigade of prisonners in the camps

kareta: a four-wheeled open carriage or cart

karpas: greenery (usually parsley) used ritually at Passover Seder

kavannah: directed attention and concentration for prayer and study

kehilah: Jewish community

Ketuba (ketubot): marriage contract, often artistically designed with ornamental calligraphy

kibbutz: collective farm in Israel

kiddush: the blessing over wine to usher in the Sabbath

Kislev: Jewish month during which Hanukkah occurs

Kol Nidre: "All vows," the major opening solemn prayer chanted on Yom Kippur Eve

Korban Mincha: literally "the sacrifice of the late afternoon," here the name of a prayer book mainly used by women

kosher: ritually appropriate

kugel: a Sabbath pudding consisting of noodles, raisins, and other ingredients

kvitl (kvitlech): slip of paper containing a request for help in spiritual matters

k'vod hameth: respect for the dead

Lagerälteste: prisoner who functioned as head of all the other prisoners in a camp

lebjoda: an edible bitter weed, often eaten by prisoners

Machzor: special prayer book for the holidays
Maoz Tzur: a favorite traditional Hanukkah song
maror: bitter herbs
matzos: unleavened bread, eaten on Passover
menorah: a seven- or eight-branch candleholder
Midrash: rabbinic interpretation of biblical texts
mikvah: ritual bath
minyan: quorum of ten men needed for public worship
Mishnah: the oldest portion of the Talmud, edited around 200 Common
    Era
Mitzrayim: Egypt
mitzvah: good deed, commandment
mizrach: decorated paper or parchment cut-out indicating the eastern
    wall of a dwelling and thus the direction of Jerusalem
Modeh-ani: the first prayer one recites on awakening
mokir-Haifa: an honored citizen of the city of Haifa

Ne'ila: concluding prayer on Yom Kippur afternoon
nudnik: bore or nuisance

pelzmantel: fur coat
Pentateuch: The five books of Moses
peyos: side-curls worn by some traditional Jewish males
phylacteries: small leather boxes with portions of scripture inside, ritu-
    ally worn at morning prayers
pritches: wooden bed bunks in the camps
protekcja: special connections
Purim: a Jewish holiday based on the book of Esther

Rassenkunde: racial (pseudo) "science" of the National Socialists
Rathaus: centrally located town hall, the main administrative building
    of a town
reb: sir, mister
rebbe: Hasidic master
Rosh Chodesh: new moon
Rosh Hashanah: New (Jewish) Year

Seder: elaborate and festive meal with symbolic food, songs, and rituals, narrating the story of the Exodus

Sefer Torah: Torah scroll

Shabbat: the sabbath

shabbos oibst: fruit handed out to students on Sabbath afternoons

shammes: beadle or sexton of a synagogue or Beis Midrash

Shavuos: "Pentecost," the anniversary of the reception of the Ten Commandments

Shema: "hear"; the first word of the recital of the Jewish faith

shofar: ram's horn

shtetl: village or town with a significant Jewish population

shul: synagogue

Simchas Torah: festival of great joy and dancing with Torah scrolls

Stasi: East German secret police

stiebel: Hasidic place of prayer and study

Sukkos: tabernacle, feast of booths

tallis: prayer shawl

tallis-kattan: small personal prayer shawl worn by observant Jewish men at all times

"Tanya": mystical text made into a song by contemporary Hasidim

tefillin: phylacteries worn by Jewish men during morning prayers

Tikun Rachel: special prayers and meditations recited at midnight, pleading for Matriarch Rachel's intercession

Tikun Leah: special prayers and meditations recited at midnight, pleading for Matriarch Leah's intervention

t'kia gedola: "the great sound" of the ram's horn at the end of the Yom Kippur afternoon service (Ne'ila), also symbolic of the coming of the Messiah and of redemption

Torah: here used in its widest meaning of learning and study

treif: ritually unclean or unfit to eat

tsedakah: charitable giving

Tsena U'rena: collection of biblical stories and commentaries designed primarily for women

tsimes: desert made of sweetened and spiced carrots

tzitzis: fringes of a prayer shawl

uberleben: survive

Vernichtungslager: death camp
Vidui: prayers of confession before death

yeshiva: Talmudic academy
Yetziv Pisgam: a poetic prayer recited on Pentecost
Yom Hashoah: the day set aside in the Jewish calendar to commemorate
     the victims of the Holocaust
Yom Kippur: Day of Atonement

zeroa: the roast lamb bone used as the symbol of the pascal lamb on the
     eve of Passover

Index

Adler, Alfred, 70
Akiba, Rabbi: martyrdom of, 79-80
Alter, Avrom Mordecai (rebbe of Ger), 85, 92
Anti-Semitic propaganda, 15-16, 17, 162
Aunt Mirele, 4
Auschwitz-Birkenau camp, 114, 128, 131-43, 168-70, 185. *See also* Concentration and slave labor camps

Ba'al Shem Tov, 3
Balut, 99
Beis Midrash, 10-12, 28, 185
Berachot, 23-24
Biebow, Hans, 102-3, 105; trial and execution of, 105
Brikman, Leibel, 94
Brother John (monk), 58-64
Brother Peter (monk), 60-64
Buber, Martin, 9

Cairo, 170
Cedar Rapids, Iowa, 179-81; Christian community and Martin Luther King Jr.'s death, 180-81
Champaign, Ill., 181
Cheder, 3-7, 8
Chevley leidah, 33-34. *See also* Messiah
Chojnice, Poland, 74
Chudi, Mottl, 155-61, 162, 174, 187
Chumash cheder, 7-8
Chumash seuda, 8
Churgin, Pinchas, 178

Cohen, Ruth, 179-81
Concentration and slave labor camps: Auschwitz-Birkenau, 114, 128, 131-43, 168-70, 185; Ebensee, 128, 150; Fünfteichen, 128, 136, 143-47; Fürstenfelde, 109, 122, 137, 142; Gross Rosen, 128, 146-49; Mauthausen, 128, 146-50, 173, 176; order in which I.N. experienced camps, 128; Poznan, 72, 109, 119, 137-40; St. Martin's, 64, 109, 122, 110-22, 123-34, 137, 139, 142, 175; Wels, 128, 150, 176; Yunikowo (Lenzingen), 110, 123, 137, 140
Constantinople, 170
Corporal punishment, 68-69

Deportations: of first group from Zdunska Wola, 109-10; first rehearsals for, 98-99; of grandmother, 50-52
Domb, Ziggi, 125-35
Dothan, Ala., 179-80
Dreams: of the coming of the Messiah, 171-72; of gold coins in St. Martin's camp, 113-14

East Berlin (GDR), 181-83
Ebelsberg, Austria, 176
Egypt, 45-46, 63, 124, 134, 168, 170, 185
Eiger, Rabbi Akiba, 112, 151
Einstadts Park (Zdunska Wola, Poland), 4

Elijah (prophet), 28, 90-91, 129, 135
Expulsion: of Polish Jews from Germany, 73-75

Fort Valley State College, Ga., 180
Frankl, Viktor, 183
Freudmann, Ester, 50, 187
Frumer, Simon, 115-16, 118, 128, 132
Fuchs, Hauptmann, 103-4

Gematria: of I.N.'s Auschwitz number, 143; of the word *shabbat*, 163-64
Gerer Hasidim, 57, 73, 98
German Reich, 37, 50
Ger, Poland, 84-86
Gerszonowicz, Srulik, 51, 68, 70, 91, 96
Gestapo, 57, 58, 78, 138
Gog and Magog, 34
Goisern, Austria, 157, 173
Gold: chalice, 47-48; coins, 112-13, 114; digging for coins, 110, 142; fillings, 111, 118; and the milk cans of Warsaw, 184-84; smuggling into Auschwitz, 141-42
Goldberg, Moischele, 111-13
Goldsmith, Jean, 178

Haggadah, 180, 185; of St. Martin's camp, 127, 133-36
Haifa, Israel, 158-61, 187
Hakhshara, 156
Haman, 63, 78, 88
Hans Pracht Hoch- und Tiefbau (construction company), 111, 117, 127, 130
Hanukkah, 55-64, 130, 164, 181
Hashomer Hatsair (Zionist youth group), 67-69; and Bronka, 67; and Hannania Grossman, 67, 69-70, 151; and Poryia, 67, 151
Havdalah, 163
Hebrew Union College, Cincinnati, 178-79, 181
Heschel, Abraham Joshua, 183
High Holy Days, 86

Hirschberg, Avrum Yiedel, 33, 36, 37, 49
Hitler, Adolf, 15, 157
Holocaust Memorial Council (U.S.), 181
Holocaust Museum (U.S.), 184

Ishmael, Rabbi Ben Elisha, 25-26

Jachimowicz, Nochem, 79
Jerusalem Certificates, 99
Jesus, 57
Jewish calendar (Goebbels), 78, 88
Joint Distribution Committee, 177-78
Judenälteste, 72, 95-105
Judenrat: duties of, 96

Kaddish: in Auschwitz-Birkenau (1987); at burial of Rabbi Akiba Eiger's name, 112; in displaced persons' camp, 176
Kalisz, Poland, 19, 20, 42, 44, 45, 49
Kapos: Lagerälteste Srulik Rosenfeld, 116-21, 123-36, 151, 174-75; Pinchas Potrzebowsky, 116-21, 123-24, 151, 174-75; Shlomo Schultz, 116-21, 123-24, 151, 174-75;
Kartus-Bereza, Poland, 41, 76
Katzenelson, Yitzhak, 94
Kehilah, 97
Kiddush Hashem, 79. *See also* Martyrdom
Kindness: of Brothers John and Peter, 57-63; of Doctor Katz, 179; individual acts of, 186; of JDC staff, 177-78; of Joel Zolna after the war, 176; of Polish cook in St. Martin's, 118-19; of Rabbi Narot, 178; Shmuel and gift of a coat, 148-49
King, Dr. Martin Luther, Jr., 180
Kol Nidre, 87
Kolo, 155
Kol Shearith Israel Synagogue, Republic of Panama, 179
Koppel, Yakov, 127, 132-36
Kracow, Poland, 3, 74, 131

Krupp Munitions Works, 143
Kvitl (kvitlech), 7, 85, 164, 171

Leib, Uren, 33, 35, 37
Lemberg, Dr. Yakov, 72, 77, 95-105,
184; and Biebow, 102-3; emigration
certificates and, 99; final days, 104-
5; as the "great Jew," 103; I.N.'s earliest memories of, 97-98; as
Judenälteste, 96-97; meeting with
Rumkowski in Lodz, 99-100; and
physicals of Isaac and Yossel Neuman, 71; prisoners from Poznan
camps and, 102; and Purim martyrs, 78-79; role in Purim hangings,
80-81; and Shavuos martyrs, 88-90
Leon (St. Martin's inmate), 131-36
Levitt, Joseph, 102, 187
Linz, Austria, 173, 175, 178
Lodz, Poland, 3, 83, 99-100, 103, 105,
185
Lublin, Poland, 3, 17

Maoz Tzur, 62-63
Marczyniak, Boleslaw, 16, 18
Martyrdom, in Zdunska Wola: first
three, 36-38; Kiddush Hashem, 79;
Purim martyrs, 83; Rabbi Akiba's
martyrdom, 79-80; Shavuos mar-
tyrs, 92
Mary (the Madonna), 57, 60, 62
Messiah, 24, "birth pangs" and the
wish not to be present at his com-
ing, 33-34, 167; the coming of, 48,
85, 90-91, 92; a song of redemp-
tion, 164-65; and the Western
Wall, 171-72
Minyan, 31, 78, 80, 81
Mitzvoh, 9, 22, 114
Monks: in Zdunska Wola, 57-64
Morgenstern, Mordecai, 88

Najdat, Dovid, 14
Narot, Rabbi Joseph, 178
National Democrats (Endecja), 15
Ne'ila, 85, 90-91, 93, 184

Neuman, Ari Mark (son of I.N.), 184
Neuman, David (son of I.N.), 180-81,
184-86
Neuman, Esther (sister of I.N.), 142,
151; and coal, 55-56, 65-66; incident of the tefillin and, 70-71
Neuman, Eva Grünstein (wife of
I.N.), 183
Neuman, Fischel (brother of I.N.),
151, 174, 185, 187
Neuman, Guitel (sister of I.N.), 55-56,
65, 70, 101, 151
Neuman Hannah Malka (sister of
I.N.), 71, 151
Neuman, Luba (sister of I.N.), 51, 71,
135, 151
Neuman, Mindel (sister of I.N.), 71,
151
Neuman, Mordecai (father of I.N.),
10; concern for I.N.'s slow develop-
ment, 7-8; description of his store,
39-40; and Dr. Lemberg, 96-97,
100; early days in the ghetto, 55-
56; and faith, 174; friendship with
Boleslaw Marczyniak, 16-17, 18, 19;
on morning of I.N.'s deportation,
70; and Reb Mendel, 20, 33-35; and
Shlomo Zelichowski, 85, 92, 94;
and Strykower rebbe, 163, 167; at
Zdunska Wola cemetery (August
1942), 103
Neuman, Rachel (mother of I.N.),
162, 174; encouragement of I.N. in
Zdunska Wola, 19; and Grandmother's shroud, 101; and I.N.'s deportation, 70; on returning home
after fleeing early in war, 35; sabbath candles incident, 9-10; at
Zdunska Wola Cemetery (August
1942), 103
Neuman, Yachet (sister of I.N.), 50,
71, 151
Neuman, Yossel (brother of I.N.), 56,
69, 87, 91, 109-22, 123-36, 137-51,
171; and Auschwitz, 141-42; on
difficulties of life in camps, 121-22,

139; as The Engineer, 67; entry into clinic, 149-50; and gold coins, 142; injury, 145-46; Krupp Munitions Works and, 143; and leather for shoes incident, 145; pact with I.N., 71; rounded up, 70-71; saving I.N.'s life, 114-18, 120-21; in St. Martin's Cemetery, 110-22; tools for baking matzohs and, 130

"Oifn Pripechok." *See* Prayers and songs
Oredownik (newspaper), 15-16, 17
Ozorowicz, Abraham, 27, 33, 36, 37, 49

Pabianice, Poland, 83, 84
Panama, 179
Paris, 156
Passover, 123-36, 181
Pick (a collaborator), 68, 96, 102, 104
Pilsudski, Marshall Josef, 162
Pogrom, 17
Polish Socialist Party, 12
Potrzebowsky, Pinchas. *See* Kapos
Poznan, Poland, 102, 119
Prayers and songs: "El-nora alilah," 93; morning prayer, 10-11; "Moscheiach Kummt Schon Bald," 165; "Oifn Pripechok," 5-7; prayer for a dying person, 148; prayer for God's return to Jerusalem, 171-72; "Soll Schon Sein, die Geulah," 164-65; Tikun Leah, 165; Tikun Rachel, 165; "T'nu Shira Vashevach La'ael Asher Shabath Barah," 164; "Veleyereushalayim ircha berachamim tashuv," 166
Przytek, Poland, 17
Purim, 72-82, 88, 92, 94
Puttermilch (Jew in Zdunska Wola), 41-42

Rabbi Joshua, 90-91
Railroads: building railroad in Fürstenfelde camp, 140; inaguration of railroad in Zdunska Wola, 22-23
Railroad stations: at Auschwitz, 141, 168; as places of deportation, 51, 94, 104-5
Rassenkunde, 66
Ravensbruck, 158
Reagan, Ronald, 181, 184
Reb Arele, 4-7
Rebbe of Strykow (the alte rebbe), 135, 162-67, 171-72; vision of Rachel, 166-67
Rebbe of Strykow (grandson of the alte rebbe), 159-60, 162
Rebbe of Zgierz. *See* Rebbe of Strykow (the alte rebbe)
Rebbe's Court (in Zgierz), 19, 34, 49, 186
Reb Mendel (Mordcha Mendel Strykowski), 10, 19-38, 96, 151, 174-75, 183-84, 188; appearance of and early life, 21-23; arrest for "conspiracy," 36-37; on "birth pangs," 33-34; on causeless hatred, 27-28; on critics and criticism, 29-31; execution of, 35-36, 37; on futility of fighting, 25-27; on how to pray when traveling, 28-29; as I.N.'s teacher, 20, 23-24; on meaning of the train, telephone, and telegraph, 22-23; on the "narrow bridge," 23; on origin of Rosh Chodesh, 32; as a peacemaker, 25; on spirituality, 25; on the virtue of silence, 31
Reb Nachman of Braslav, 23, 141, 150, 174
Reb Sender, 55, 70
Reilla (woman in Zdunska Wola), 12-14
Rogozinski, Leib, 76-77, 81-82
Rosenfeld, Srulik. *See* Kapos
Rosh Chodesh, 32
Rosh Hashanah, 84
Rudal, Benjamin, 83, 87, 88
Rumkowski, Chaim, 99-100, 101

Sabbath, 9-10, 10-15, 42-44; and lighting candles for, 43-45; Rabbi Akiba's observation of, 79-80; in Zdunska Wola, 137
Satan, 27, 48
Schneidholz and Son, 74, 76
Schor, Moischele (Maury), 102, 187
Schultz, Shlomo, 116, 120-21
Seder: preparations for in St. Martin's, 123-36
Selma, Ala., march, 180
Shavuos, 88-94
Shema, 80
Shmuel (Mauthausen inmate), 146-49, 151, 173, 180
Shor, Moschele, 187
Shtetl: defined, 3
Sieradz, 98
Simchas Torah, 103
Sinai Temple, Champaign, Ill., 181
Sittner, Jakob, 122; accusal of stealing bread, 138; execution of, 139; reputation as baker, 137
Stasi (East German Secret Police), 182
Stiebel, 10, 22, 25, 29, 31, 34, 71, 113; Fisherman's Stiebel, Haifa, 160
Strykowski, Mordcha Mendel. *See* Reb Mendel
Survival (physical): extra food, 119; I.N. as "gardener" in Fünfteichen, 144-45; I.N. and gathering coal, 56-57, 61; I.N. and stealing leather for shoes, 145; price of potatoes and, 120-22
Survival (spiritual): and acts of kindness, 186; as a duty, 119-20, 148-49, 173; the milk cans of Warsaw, 184-85; Seder in St. Martin's, 135-36
Szevczik (Polish supervisor in St. Martin's camp), 126-27, 130, 133
Szmulevicz, Poryia. *See* Hashomer Hatsair

Talmud, 28-29, 33, 36, 39
Tel Aviv, Israel, 160

Temple Emanue-El, Dothan, Ala., 179
Temple Judah, Cedar Rapids, Iowa, 179
Traskalawski, Haskel, 10-15
Tyger, Aunt Fruma, 119, 187
Tyger, Masha (grandmother of I.N.), 39-52, 55, 62, 70, 91, 184-85; "conversation" with God, 43-44; deportation of, 50-52; and I.N., 49; incident of her shroud, 101; and I.N.'s father, 39-40; Mottl Chudi and, 156-57; and Puttermilch, 41-42; view of the Joseph story, 45-46

University of Cincinnati, 179

Vietnam War, 180-81

Warsaw, 3, 49, 184, 185, 186
Western Wall: midrashic view of origin, 172
Wiesel, Elie, 183

Yeshiva, 19, 45, 60, 155
Yeshiva College, New York, 178
Yeshiva Emek-halacha, Warsaw, 19, 34
Yom Hashoah, 173-86
Yom Kippur, 84-85, 89, 90-91, 184
Yossi (Rabbi), 28
Yunikowo (Lenzingen) camp: I.N.'s arrival at, 110

Zalmen (boy in Zdunska Wola), 20, 23, 29
Zbonszyn, Poland, 74
Zelichokwski, Schlomo, 72, 83-94, 95, 135, 174, 181, 183-84; arrest of, 88; and "El-nora alilah," 93; fame of, 84; hanging of, 93-94; move to Zdunska Wola, 84; preparation for the gallows, 89-92; and the shofar, 85-86, 92; "Song of Shlomo Zelichowski," 94
Zelichowski, Zelda, 84-88

Zgierz, Poland, 19, 35, 49, 183, 185, 186

Zilberberg, Nochem Ellia, 72-82, 184; arrest of, 77-78; on dying with dignity and courage, 79; execution of, 80-82; expulsion from Germany, 74; life in Germany, 73-74; as manager of Schneidholz and Son, 74-77; personal qualities of, 72-73; transformation into a penitent, 76-77; work as a strike-breaker, 75

Zillia (Mottl Chudi's love), 157-61

Zionism, 33-34, 156-57, 182,

Zolna, Joel, 176

ISAAC NEUMAN attended rabbinic academies in Kalisz and Warsaw before his deportion in May 1941 to the first of several labor camps and concentration camps. He was liberated by the Eightieth Infantry Division of the U.S. Army on May 5, 1945, and spent several years in hospitals and rehabilitation centers in Austria before arriving in the United States in 1950. He received a B.A. and an M.A. of Hebrew Letters, his rabbinical ordination, and an honorary doctorate of divinity from Hebrew Union College. He served as the rabbi of the Kol Shearith Israel Congregation in the Republic of Panama and at Temple Judah in Cedar Rapids, Iowa, and Sinai Temple in Champaign, Illinois. In 1987–88 he served as the first rabbi of East Berlin in the postwar years. He has also taught and published widely, as well as participated in planning the U.S. Holocaust Museum.

MICHAEL PALENCIA-ROTH, born in Girardot, Colombia, obtained a B.A. in English and philosophy from Vanderbilt University and an M.A. and Ph.D. in comparative literature from Harvard University. A professor of comparative literature, Spanish, and Latin American Studies at the University of Illinois, his work covers a wide variety of topies, including German literature and thought, English literature, Latin American literature, and contemporary Colombian culture. In June 1998 he was decorated with the Order of Merit in Art and Culture Pedro Morales Pino for his contributions to Colombian letters.

Typeset in 9.5/14 Stone Serif
with Triplex display
Designed by Paula Newcomb
Composed by Barbara Evans
at the University of Illinois Press
Manufactured by Thomson-Shore, Inc.

University of Illinois Press
1325 South Oak Street
Champaign, IL 61820-6903
www.press.uillinois.edu